TOBACCO TALES

Tobacco Tales

From Leaf to Lungs

ALINA HAZLE

Spectra Enterprise

Contents

Table Of Content   1

Introduction   3

Chapter 1   5

Chapter 2   13

Chapter 3   24

Chapter 4   39

Chapter 5   50

Chapter 6   64

Chapter 7   77

Chapter 8   91

Chapter 9   104

Chapter 10   120

Table Of Content

Introduction

Chapter 1: The Origins of a Leaf
1.1 Explore the historical roots of tobacco cultivation and its cultural significance.
1.2 Discuss the early uses of tobacco by indigenous peoples and its introduction to the wider world.

Chapter 2: The Rise of Smoking
2.1 Trace the evolution of smoking habits, from pipes and cigars to the ubiquitous cigarette.
2.2 Examine the societal changes that accompanied the widespread adoption of tobacco.

Chapter 3: The Science Behind Addiction
3.1 Dive into the chemistry of tobacco and the addictive properties of nicotine.
3.2 Discuss the psychological and physiological effects of smoking on the human body.

Chapter 4: Tobacco Industry Tactics
4.1 Investigate the strategies employed by the tobacco industry in marketing and advertising.
4.2 Explore the controversial history of tobacco companies and their impact on public health.

Chapter 5: The Battle for Regulation

5.1 Chart the efforts to regulate tobacco, from early warnings to present-day policies.

5.2 Explore the challenges faced by governments and public health organizations in curbing tobacco use.

Chapter 6: Tobacco and Health

6.1 Examine the direct health consequences of smoking, including respiratory diseases and cancer.

6.2 Discuss secondhand smoke and the impact of smoking on overall public health.

Chapter 7: Quitting the Habit

7.1 Explore the various methods and challenges of quitting smoking.

7.2 Share personal stories of individuals who successfully kicked the habit.

Chapter 8: The Global Tobacco Epidemic

8.1 Investigate the worldwide impact of tobacco use on different cultures and societies.

8.2 Discuss the efforts of international organizations to combat the global tobacco epidemic.

Chapter 9: Innovations and Alternatives

9.1 Explore emerging technologies and alternative products designed to reduce harm.

9.2 Discuss the controversy and potential benefits of products like e-cigarettes and smokeless tobacco.

Chapter 10: Towards a Smoke-Free Future

10.1 Summarize the progress made in reducing tobacco use globally.

10.2 Explore future trends and potential solutions to create a smoke-free world.

Introduction

In the many-sided embroidery of mankind's set of experiences, scarcely any substances have woven a story as perplexing, questionable, and unavoidable as tobacco. "Tobacco Stories: From Leaf to Lungs" leaves on an excursion through time, disentangling the complex strings that tight spot this unassuming leaf to the texture of social orders across the globe. Our investigation starts in the fog of ancient history, where native societies originally developed and used tobacco for ceremonial and restorative purposes.

As we cross through the hallways of time, the account unfurls with the ascent of smoking, following the transformation from lines and stogies to the notorious cigarette that would become inseparable from the actual demonstration. This story isn't restricted to the rich tobacco fields or the faintly lit corners of smoking parlors; it reaches out to the actual center of our science. In the research facility of science, we dig into the unpredictable science of tobacco, taking apart the habit-forming properties of nicotine that tight spot people to this antiquated plant.

At the same time, we turn our look to the passages of force and impact, analyzing the tobacco business' impressive strategies in showcasing and promoting, frequently covered in discussion and pushing the limits of morals. The call for guideline reverberations through the pages as we examine the fight between general wellbeing and benefit, researching the advancing scene of tobacco control endeavors and the enduring battle against an industry that has blossomed with compulsion.

As the air clears, the account turns to the actual main issue - the significant effect of tobacco on human wellbeing. Past the actual cost, we investigate the mental complexities that make breaking liberated from tobacco's grip a strenuous excursion. This book isn't only a report; it is a demonstration of flexibility and the human soul's ability for change. Our investigation isn't restricted to boundaries or societies; it extends across mainlands, pondering the worldwide tobacco pestilence and the aggregate endeavors to relieve its ramifications.

With an eye toward the future, we review the scene of developments and choices, thinking about the commitments and traps of arising advancements intended to lessen hurt. In the end parts, the story turns hopeful as we imagine a sans smoke future, drawing on the aggregate insight collected from the former pages to enlighten possible ways ahead. "Tobacco Stories: From Leaf to Lungs" is in excess of a verifiable record; it is an odyssey through the social, logical, and socio-political components of tobacco.

It is an encouragement to draw in with a point that rises above time, testing predispositions, and offering a nuanced comprehension of an element that has, no matter what, made a permanent imprint on the human experience. As we leave on this scholarly excursion, let the pages of this book spread out like ringlets of smoke, uncovering the unpredictable stories and significant illustrations laced inside the universe of tobacco.

Chapter 1

The Origins of a Leaf

In the chronicles of organic history, there exists a leaf that has charmed civilizations, woven into the texture of ceremonies, and made a permanent imprint on the human experience — the tobacco leaf. To leave on the excursion of understanding the starting points of this modest leaf is to explore through the halls of time, following the earliest associations among people and Nicotiana, the class to which tobacco has a place. Our story starts in the pre-Columbian Americas, where native societies originally developed and saddled the capability of this plant.

The utilization of tobacco by local people groups originates before written history, with archeological proof recommending that tobacco has been important for human ceremonies for millennia. Native people group, from North America to South America, worshipped the tobacco plant for its profound importance, integrating it into services, contributions, and mending rehearses. Tobacco was not simply a ware; it was a conductor to the heavenly, a medium through which correspondence with the other-worldly domain was worked with. The smoke drifting from copying tobacco leaves was accepted to convey messages and petitions to the sky.

The development and use of tobacco by Local American clans like the Cherokee, Iroquois, and Powhatan were profoundly entwined with their social and strict practices. The tobacco plant held a consecrated status, frequently representing decontamination and association with the profound world. Its passes on were utilized in services to look for direction, offer thanks, or summon assurance. The multifaceted customs encompassing the development, gathering, and utilization of tobacco highlighted its significance in the social embroidered artwork of these native social orders.

As European travelers set forth in the Period of Disclosure, they experienced new universes and new vegetation, including the strange tobacco plant. Christopher Columbus is attributed with acquainting tobacco with Europe after his journeys to the Americas, in spite of the fact that its reception was at first sluggish. It was only after the mid sixteenth century that tobacco acquired ubiquity in European circles, prodded by the compositions of Spanish pioneers like Hernán Cortés and the French representative Jean Nicot. As a matter of fact, the variety Nicotiana is named after Nicot, who sent tobacco seeds and passes on to the French court, praising their restorative ethics.

The groundbreaking excursion of tobacco went on as it crossed seas and societies, turning into a worldwide peculiarity. The reception of tobacco smoking spread quickly, rising above borders and cultural limits. In the Ottoman Realm, the act of smoking tobacco in water lines, or hookahs, acquired prominence. In Asia, especially in Japan and China, tobacco turned into a necessary piece of social and social traditions.

The appeal of tobacco arrived at the shores of North America with the foundation of the main English settlements. Tobacco development turned into a foundation of the financial reasonability of repayments like Jamestown in Virginia, where the money crop gave a worthwhile product to European business sectors. The development of tobacco, in any case, was not without its difficulties, as the requests for work in tobacco fields laid the basis for the foundation of subjugation.

Tobacco's impact stretched out past the Americas and Europe, tracking down its direction to the Center East, Africa, and Asia through the multifaceted snare of shipping lanes that confounded the globe. The trading of tobacco became interwoven with the more extensive trade of products, thoughts, and societies during a period of investigation and globalization.

The tobacco plant's excursion from sacrosanct customs in native social orders to a worldwide product was set apart by shifts in discernment and reason. What started as a profound conductor developed into a business venture, everlastingly changing the connection among people and this baffling leaf. As tobacco turned out to be progressively commodified, it changed from a holy spice to a sought-after monetary asset, with its development forming scenes and economies.

The starting points of the tobacco leaf are not bound to a particular locale; they spread across landmasses, it is both rich and complex to make a verifiable mosaic that. The tale of tobacco is one of social trade, variation, and change, mirroring the complex interchange among humankind and the normal world. As we dive into the starting points of this leaf, we disentangle the layers of history, from the holy services of native people groups to the clamoring shipping lanes that worked with the worldwide spread of tobacco.

In following the excursion of the tobacco leaf, it becomes obvious that its story is joined with the more extensive embroidered artwork of mankind's set of experiences. The starting points of a leaf rise above the herbal; they include the otherworldly, the financial, and the social elements of the human experience. As we investigate the beginning of tobacco, we strip back the layers of time, uncovering the intricacies and inconsistencies implanted throughout the entire existence of a leaf that has left a persevering through engrave on our reality.

1.1 Explore the historical roots of tobacco cultivation and its cultural significance.

Setting out on an excursion through the verifiable underlying foundations of tobacco development is similar to venturing into the chronicles of time, where the ringlets of Nicotiana, the class to which tobacco has a place, first flourished in the social soil of old civilizations. The story unfurls in the fruitful scenes of the pre-Columbian Americas, where native people groups developed and adored the tobacco plant for its complex importance.

In the rich scopes of North and South America, Local American clans like the Cherokee, Powhatan, and Iroquois became stewards of tobacco, perceiving its profound strength. Tobacco was not simply a plant; it was a conductor to the heavenly. Native people group participated in mind boggling customs encompassing the development, collecting, and utilization of tobacco, implanting it with significant social and strict importance. The smoke ascending from copying tobacco leaves was accepted to convey supplications to the otherworldly domain, producing an association between the natural and the heavenly.

As we navigate the authentic scene, the sacrosanct idea of tobacco in native societies turns out to be progressively evident. The Cherokee, for example, saw tobacco as a hallowed gift from the Incomparable Soul, integrating it into services to offer thanks, look for direction, and conjure insurance. The Iroquois, known for their modern agrarian practices, developed tobacco as an essential piece of their horticultural and otherworldly customs. In the Powhatan Alliance, tobacco assumed a focal part in services and customs, representing refinement and fellowship with the powerful.

The social meaning of tobacco stretched out past the otherworldly domain; it penetrated social and shared elements. Tobacco filled in as a mode of trade and gift-giving among Local American clans, encouraging unions and reinforcing social bonds. Its stately use turned into a shared encounter, building up the texture of native social orders and epitomizing an agreeable connection among people and nature.

The experience between native societies and European travelers in the late fifteenth century denoted a critical second in the worldwide dissemination of tobacco. Christopher Columbus, after arriving at the Americas, experienced the native act of smoking tobacco and noticed its formal importance. The voyagers who continued afterward, including Hernán Cortés and Jean Nicot, assumed instrumental parts in acquainting tobacco with European crowds.

The dispersion of tobacco across landmasses was joined by a change in its discernment and use. In Europe, tobacco at first built up momentum for its implied restorative properties. Jean Nicot, the French diplomat to Portugal, sent tobacco seeds and passes on to the French court, supporting for its restorative advantages. The sort Nicotiana is named in his honor, mirroring his job in advocating tobacco in European circles.

Tobacco's excursion from the consecrated customs of native societies to the courts of Europe highlighted its versatility and ability to rise above social limits. The shift from a profound channel to a restorative product denoted a defining moment in the direction of tobacco, making way for its commodification and worldwide scattering.

The sixteenth and seventeenth hundreds of years saw the foundation of tobacco as a money crop in the English settlements of North America. In Virginia, Jamestown arose as a point of convergence for tobacco development, and the monetary practicality of the repayment turned out to be characteristically connected to the development and commodity of tobacco. The interest for work in tobacco fields laid the basis for the establishment of bondage, as African workers were effectively brought to the provinces to work in the tobacco manors.

Tobacco's development became inseparable from financial success, molding the scenes and social orders of the states. The tobacco exchange blossomed, making financial conditions that resonated across the Atlantic. The financial progress of tobacco ranches energized the extension of European settlements in the Americas and added to the advancement of the overseas exchange organizations.

The social meaning of tobacco went through additional change as it became interwoven with the new economies of the New World. Tobacco turned into a money of trade, an image of riches, and a product that formed social orders. The tobacco estate, with its rambling fields and work escalated development, turned into a characterizing element of the Southern US, forming the locale's set of experiences and personality.

As we explore through the verifiable underlying foundations of tobacco development, it becomes clear that the excursion of this leaf is an embroidery woven with strings of culture, otherworldliness, and financial matters. The consecrated customs of native people groups cross with the monetary objectives of European provinces, it is both complicated and interconnected to make a story that. The tobacco plant, when a holy course in the ceremonies of Local American clans, went through a transformation as it navigated seas and societies, adjusting to new settings and getting different layers of importance.

Amidst this authentic investigation, recognizing the significant effect of tobacco development on human societies is critical. The monetary progress of tobacco estates came at a significant expense, as the interest for work prompted the ruthless double-dealing of oppressed people. The dull shadow of the transoceanic slave exchange poses a potential threat over the historical backdrop of tobacco, highlighting the intricacies and moral situations implanted in its development.

The worldwide dispersion of tobacco didn't happen in disconnection; it unfurled inside the more extensive setting of expansionism, exchange, and social trade. Tobacco turned into a ware that rose above borders, forming worldwide economies and impacting social designs. Its development made a permanent imprint on scenes, both physical and social, as tobacco fields became meaningful of monetary thriving and, all the while, the dull tradition of abuse.

In investigating the verifiable underlying foundations of tobacco development, it is fundamental to defy the intricacies of its set of experiences — a set of experiences that entwines the hallowed with the profane, the profound with the financial. The tobacco leaf, when an image of fellowship with the heavenly in the ceremonies of native societies, transformed into a worldwide item that would shape the predeterminations of countries. As we dig into this multi-layered story, we are constrained to go up against the social meaning of tobacco as well as the moral components of its authentic direction.

The verifiable underlying foundations of tobacco development, perplexing and diverse, entice us to consider the interconnectedness of human social orders and the extraordinary force of an apparently basic leaf. The tobacco plant, with its beginnings in the consecrated customs of native people groups, set out on an excursion that crossed landmasses, traversed hundreds of years, and left a getting through engrave on the worldwide scene. The investigation of this verifiable embroidery is a challenge to wrestle with the subtleties of social trade, financial double-dealing, and the persevering through tradition of a leaf that, no matter what, became laced with the human story.

1.2 Discuss the early uses of tobacco by indigenous peoples and its introduction to the wider world.

Leaving on a significant investigation of the early purposes of tobacco by native people groups is similar to diving into the old sections of social history, where the tobacco plant arose as a hallowed and multi-layered element in the customs and practices of Local American clans. The story unfurls in the unblemished scenes of the pre-Columbian Americas, where the native development of tobacco rose above simple cultivation; it turned into a consecrated fellowship with the normal world and the heavenly.

The beginnings of tobacco as a stylized and formal substance are well established in the profound acts of Local American clans. Tobacco, organically delegated Nicotiana, was developed with care and veneration by native networks across North and South America. The Cherokee, Iroquois, Powhatan, and incalculable different clans viewed tobacco as a sacrosanct gift from the Incomparable Soul, crediting significant other-worldly importance to the plant.

In the profound scene of Local American societies, tobacco turned into a channel for correspondence with the heavenly. The demonstration of smoking or copying tobacco leaves held profound ceremonial significance, and the smoke was accepted to convey supplications and messages to the otherworldly domain. Tobacco was utilized in services to offer thanks, look for direction, and summon security. The Cherokee, for example, held hallowed services where tobacco was presented as a token of appreciation to the Incomparable Soul for the abundance of the land.

The Iroquois, known for their refined farming practices, developed tobacco as a component of their agrarian and profound customs. Tobacco was incorporated into customs and services, representing filtration and the foundation of an otherworldly association. The Powhatan Alliance comparatively participated in stately tobacco use, thinking of it as a method for speaking with the powerful powers that represented their reality.

The stately utilization of tobacco was not bound to explicit events; it pervaded the day to day routines of native people groups. The shared demonstration of passing around a stately line loaded up with tobacco cultivated social securities and supported the interconnectedness of people inside the local area. The meaning of tobacco stretched out past the actual demonstration of smoking; it turned into a social and social cement, meshing its direction into the texture of native social orders.

As European pilgrims set out on their excursions of revelation in the late fifteenth hundred years, they experienced the consecrated works on encompassing tobacco in the New World. Christopher Columbus, after arriving at the Americas, saw the native people groups smoking tobacco and noticed its formal importance. Be that as it may, the early European pioneers didn't promptly get a handle on the otherworldly profundity of tobacco's job in native societies.

The groundbreaking second in the worldwide scattering of tobacco happened when wayfarers, for example, Hernán Cortés and Jean Nicot perceived the capability of tobacco past its stately use. Cortés, in his experiences with the Aztecs, noticed the Aztec sovereign Moctezuma enjoying the smoking of tobacco. The act of smoking, recently viewed as a consecrated custom, started to obtain various implications as it converged with the Europeans' interest in new substances from the Americas.

Jean Nicot, the French minister to Portugal, assumed an essential part in acquainting tobacco with European crowds. Nicot got tobacco seeds and leaves from the New World and, perceiving their restorative potential, sent them to the French court. The expression "nicotine" is gotten from Nicot's name, a demonstration of his impact in promoting the utilization of tobacco in Europe.

The acquaintance of tobacco with Europe denoted a huge change in its discernment and use. While the hallowed customs of native societies commended the otherworldly elements of tobacco, Europe embraced it for its implied restorative properties. Tobacco was at first hailed as a panacea, accepted to fix a bunch of illnesses, from cerebral pains to toothaches. The restorative standing of tobacco became settled in European culture, establishing the groundwork for its boundless reception.

Tobacco's excursion from the sacrosanct services of native people groups to the dignified salons of Europe is significant of its versatility and pliability. The plant, at first worshipped for its profound importance, transformed into a restorative ware that caught the creative mind of European social orders. The early experiences between native purposes and European discernments set up for the intricate and complex history of tobacco on the worldwide stage.

The dispersion of tobacco across mainlands was not a unidirectional cycle; it included a corresponding trade of thoughts, practices, and discernments. The acquaintance of tobacco with the more extensive world turned into a demonstration of the interconnectedness of human social orders during the Period of Investigation. As tobacco crossed seas and rose above social limits, it conveyed with it the reverberations of native ceremonies and the expanding interest of Europeans in the colorful and novel.

The social trade that went with the spread of tobacco delivered a combination of different viewpoints and practices. In the New World, tobacco stayed a hallowed and essential piece of native societies, proceeding to be woven into the texture of functions and mutual life. In Europe, it went through a change from a restorative interest to a sporting and social guilty pleasure.

The ascent of tobacco as a worldwide ware was joined by a thriving exchange network that associated the Old World with the New. The interest for tobacco expanded, prompting the foundation of estates in the settlements of the Americas. The financial elements of tobacco development became laced with the more extensive designs of expansionism and exchange, forming the predeterminations of countries and making a permanent imprint on the verifiable scene.

As we dive into the early purposes of tobacco by native people groups and first experience with the more extensive world, it becomes obvious that the story is one of significant social crossing points and changes. The hallowed acts of native societies, established in a profound association with the regular world, experienced the curious look of European travelers looking for new skylines. The plant that once filled in as an otherworldly course in the consecrated ceremonies of Local American clans wound up relocated into the shifted scenes of Europe, where its purposes and implications went through a transformation.

The authentic embroidery woven by tobacco is unpredictable, set apart by the interlacing strings of otherworldliness, medication, exchange, and social trade. The early purposes of tobacco by native people groups, saturated with veneration and service, reverberation through time as a demonstration of the unpredictable connections among people and the plant world. At the same time, the acquaintance of tobacco with the more extensive world uncovers the dynamism of social experiences and the extraordinary force of a straightforward leaf that crossed landmasses, leaving a getting through engrave on the worldwide story.

Chapter 2

The Rise of Smoking

Setting out on an investigation of the ascent of smoking is likened to following the development of a propensity that rose above time and societies, making a permanent imprint on the human experience. This excursion navigates through hundreds of years, from the early acts of smoking lines and stogies to the far and wide reception of the notorious cigarette, unwinding the social, social, and monetary powers that formed the rising of smoking.

The underlying foundations of smoking can be followed back to old times when native societies participated in the formal and stylized utilization of tobacco. The demonstration of breathing in smoke, frequently delivered by consuming tobacco leaves in pipes or different gadgets, held profound and representative importance. The smoke was accepted to convey petitions to the heavenly, filling in as a course between the natural and profound domains. This early type of smoking was saturated with custom and custom, giving a shared and profound experience.

As the world extended through investigation and exchange, so too did the act of smoking. The experience between the native smoking practices of the Americas and European wayfarers in the fifteenth century denoted a crucial second in the worldwide dissemination of smoking. European powers, captivated by the colorful acts of the New World, started to take on and adjust the demonstration of smoking into their own societies.

The acquaintance of tobacco with Europe by wayfarers like Christopher Columbus, Hernán Cortés, and Jean Nicot started a social trade that would rethink the idea of smoking. Tobacco, at first met with interest for its restorative properties, before long turned into a sporting guilty pleasure.

The demonstration of smoking developed from a holy custom in native societies to a relaxed pursuit embraced by the European world class.

The seventeenth century saw the boundless reception of smoking across different sections of European culture. Smoking became related with refinement and status, with intricate smoking contraptions and frill becoming popular accessories among the privileged. The smoking of lines and stogies became dug in friendly customs, frequently going with conversations in cafés and salons.

The appeal of smoking rose above friendly classes, as the propensity spread from the nobility to the regular workers. Tobacco turned into a rewarding product, and its development in the settlements of the Americas filled the monetary motors of European powers. The commercialization of tobacco added to the standardization of smoking, making it an essential piece of day to day existence.

The Modern Upset additionally catalyzed the ascent of smoking. With the coming of large scale manufacturing, cigarettes arose as a helpful and open type of tobacco utilization. The motorization of cigarette creation in the late nineteenth century prepared for the democratization of smoking, making it reasonable and promptly accessible to a more extensive populace.

The defining moment throughout the entire existence of smoking accompanied the boundless fame of the cigarette in the mid twentieth hundred years. The presentation of the cutting edge cigarette, with its normalized size and shape, denoted a takeoff from conventional types of smoking. Cigarette smoking was not generally restricted to ceremonies or exceptional events; it turned into a regular practice, profoundly incorporated into the structure holding the system together.

The showcasing and promoting systems utilized by tobacco organizations assumed a critical part in the ascent of cigarette smoking. The business made complex missions that related smoking with ideas of opportunity, charm, and advancement. Notorious figures and Hollywood stars were enrolled to support cigarettes, making an optimistic picture that reverberated with buyers.

The mid-twentieth century saw an outstanding expansion in cigarette utilization, energized by variables like the finish of The Second Great War and the post-war period of prosperity. Smoking became imbued in mainstream society, highlighted conspicuously in motion pictures, promotions, and, surprisingly, clinical supports. The view of smoking as a socially OK and glitzy movement arrived at its pinnacle.

Nonetheless, as smoking arrived at its top in prominence, a counter-story arose. The 1960s and 1970s saw a developing consciousness of the wellbeing chances related with smoking. Logical exploration connected smoking to different respiratory illnesses and, most strikingly, cellular breakdown in the lungs. The Top health spokesperson's Report in the US in 1964 denoted a turning point, formally acknowledging the risks of smoking and provoking general wellbeing mediations.

The ascent of smoking, when powered by social patterns and financial interests, started to confront difficulties from a prospering enemy of smoking development. Wellbeing support gatherings, logical examination, and public mindfulness crusades intended to instruct general society about the hindering impacts of smoking. Smoking boycotts out in the open spaces, limitations on publicizing, and expanded tax assessment on tobacco items were among the actions carried out to control smoking rates.

As the twentieth century advanced into the 21st 100 years, the story around smoking went through a huge shift. The marvelousness and charm related with smoking gave way to a more nuanced comprehension of its ramifications. Legislatures overall executed severe tobacco control measures, and smoking rates started to decrease in many created nations.

The ascent of smoking, with its unpredictable exchange of social, financial, and general wellbeing factors, remains as a demonstration of the intricacy of human ways of behaving and cultural standards. The development from hallowed ceremonies in native societies to a globalized industry set apart by large scale manufacturing and complex promoting mirrors the powerful idea of smoking's climb. The resulting acknowledgment of its wellbeing gambles and the following endeavors to check its predominance feature the continuous pressure between individual decisions and general wellbeing goals.

The tradition of smoking is profoundly implanted in the verifiable embroidery of social orders across the globe. It is an account of social trade, monetary interests, and moving insights. The ascent of smoking, once inseparable from refinement and opportunity, is presently seen from the perspective of general wellbeing, with endeavors zeroed in on lessening its effect on people and networks. As we think about the excursion of smoking through the ages, it prompts us to ponder the intricate transaction of culture, trade, and wellbeing that shapes the direction of cultural propensities.

2.1 Trace the evolution of smoking habits, from pipes and cigars to the ubiquitous cigarette.

Following the development of smoking propensities is an excursion through time, a verifiable odyssey that explores the moving scenes of culture, innovation, and business. A story unfurls in the fragrant twists of smoke from lines and stogies, step by step changing into the unavoidable murkiness of the universal cigarette. This excursion typifies the unique connection among people and tobacco, from antiquated customs to the advanced period, offering bits of knowledge into the complex components of smoking propensities.

The starting points of smoking are well established in the hallowed customs of native people groups, where the demonstration of breathing in the smoke of consuming tobacco leaves held otherworldly importance. Smoking was a mind boggling piece of public ceremonies, a holy conductor between the natural and profound domains. This early type of smoking included pipes, frequently created from materials like mud or stone, and stogies produced using moved tobacco leaves. The smoke filled in as a medium to convey petitions, offer thanks, and fashion an association with the heavenly.

As the experience between native smoking customs and European pioneers unfurled, the act of smoking went through an extraordinary excursion. European powers, entranced by the colorful acts of the New World, started to take on and adjust smoking into their own societies. The acquaintance of tobacco with Europe in the fifteenth century denoted the mixture of another custom into European social orders, one that would advance throughout the long term.

In the seventeenth 100 years, smoking took on another aspect in Europe as it became related with complexity and status. The smoking of lines and stogies turned into an image of distinguished relaxation, with intricate smoking contraptions and embellishments becoming popular among the tip top. The formal idea of smoking persevered, as it went with conversations in cafés and salons, further setting its place in friendly customs.

The appeal of smoking, in any case, was not restricted to the nobility. Tobacco's commercialization and the moderateness of lines and stogies permitted smoking to rise above friendly classes. The propensity penetrated different layers of European culture, turning into a basic piece of day to day existence. The Modern Unrest assumed a crucial part in this democratization of smoking, as large scale manufacturing made lines and stogies more open to a more extensive populace.

The nineteenth century saw critical developments in smoking innovation, making way for the rise of the cutting edge cigarette. The moving machine, concocted by James Albert Bonsack in 1880, robotized the most common way of moving cigarettes, making them more reliable in size and shape. This mechanical headway denoted a shift from the work serious creation of stogies and lines to the normalized large scale manufacturing of cigarettes.

The cigarette's ascendance to conspicuousness was advanced quickly by a few variables, including its comfort, moderateness, and the changing social elements of the twentieth 100 years. Cigarettes turned into the favored type of tobacco utilization, typifying a takeoff from the stylized and relaxed nature of lines and stogies. The reduced and compact nature of cigarettes engaged a quickly urbanizing society, where existence were progressively obliged.

The promoting and publicizing procedures utilized by tobacco organizations assumed a significant part in the ascent of the cigarette. The business made complex missions that related smoking with ideas of opportunity, marvelousness, and innovation. Notorious figures and Hollywood stars were enrolled to embrace cigarettes, making an optimistic picture that reverberated with shoppers. The cigarette, with its relationship with defiance and refinement, turned into a social image, further cementing its place in the public eye.

The mid-twentieth century denoted the peak of cigarette smoking, with utilization rates arriving at remarkable levels. Cigarette smoking turned out to be profoundly imbued in mainstream society, highlighted unmistakably in films, commercials, and, surprisingly, clinical supports. The view of smoking as a socially OK and charming action was at its pinnacle.

Notwithstanding, as smoking arrived at its zenith of prominence, a counter-story arose. The 1960s and 1970s saw a developing consciousness of the wellbeing gambles related with smoking. Logical examination connected smoking to different respiratory illnesses, cardiovascular issues, and, most prominently, cellular breakdown in the lungs. The Top health spokesperson's Report in the US in 1964 denoted a turning point, formally acknowledging the risks of smoking and provoking general wellbeing mediations.

The familiarity with wellbeing gambles with started a change in cultural mentalities toward smoking. Legislatures overall carried out rigid tobacco control measures, and smoking rates started to decrease in many created nations. Smoking boycotts out in the open spaces, limitations on publicizing, and expanded tax collection on tobacco items were among the actions pointed toward controling smoking.

The advancement of smoking propensities, from lines and stogies to the omnipresent cigarette, is symbolic of the powerful transaction between culture, innovation, and industry. What started as a consecrated custom in native societies changed into an efficiently manufactured and showcased ware, formed by the powers of globalization and modernization.

The cigarette, with its relationship with disobedience and refinement, became both a social image and a general wellbeing challenge.

The downfall of smoking in ongoing many years mirrors a moving worldview in cultural standards and values. Smoking, once inseparable from style and cultural acknowledgment, is progressively seen from the perspective of general wellbeing. The story of smoking propensities is presently not exclusively one of social advancement; it is currently weaved with the basic to address the wellbeing results related with tobacco use.

The excursion of smoking propensities, from lines and stogies to the omnipresent cigarette, prompts reflection on the intricacies of human way of behaving, cultural standards, and the impact of industry. It shows the pliability of social practices notwithstanding mechanical advancements and the force of promoting. Also, the developing perspectives toward smoking highlight the continuous strain between individual decisions and general wellbeing objectives.

As we examine the direction of smoking propensities, obviously this story isn't one of straight movement yet rather an embroidery woven with strings of custom, development, and mindfulness. The historical backdrop of smoking is a demonstration of the steadily changing elements of human social orders and the complicated connection among culture and business. In the continuous mission to comprehend and address smoking propensities, the excursion from lines and stogies to the pervasive cigarette fills in as a rich and nuanced part in the more extensive story of mankind's set of experiences.

2.2 Examine the societal changes that accompanied the widespread adoption of tobacco.

Inspecting the cultural changes that went with the broad reception of tobacco is a journey through the mind boggling embroidery of mankind's set of experiences, uncovering the significant effect of this modest leaf on societies, economies, and social designs. As tobacco rose above its beginnings in native customs to turn into a worldwide product, it introduced a large group of groundbreaking changes, forming the actual texture of social orders across the world.

The coming of boundless tobacco use in the seventeenth century denoted a change in cultural standards, as smoking turned into an omnipresent practice across different fragments of European culture. Smoking, at first connected with privileged recreation, steadily penetrated through various social classes, separating conventional hindrances. The demonstration of smoking turned into a common encounter, cultivating a feeling of fellowship and shared characteristic among people from different foundations.

The rise of smoking as a social movement prompted the foundation of committed spaces where people could assemble to enjoy this freshly discovered propensity. Cafés, salons, and later, smoking parlors became scenes where individuals congregated to share discussions, thoughts, and, obviously, smoke. These spaces became pots of scholarly trade and social cooperation, adding to the prospering of the Edification and other social developments.

Tobacco likewise assumed an essential part in molding orientation elements inside society. In the beginning phases of tobacco reception, smoking was essentially connected with men, reflecting and building up existing orientation standards. Be that as it may, as cultural mentalities advanced, ladies started to participate in smoking, testing conventional orientation jobs. The cigarette, with its relationship with freedom and disobedience, turned into an image of ladies' liberation during the suffragette development and the mid twentieth 100 years.

The financial effect of inescapable tobacco development and exchange was fantastic, essentially modifying the financial scenes of areas where it flourished. The development of tobacco turned into a main thrust in the economies of the American states, especially in districts like Virginia, where tobacco manors flourished. The interest for work in these manors assumed a critical part in the foundation and development of servitude, making a getting through imprint on the social and racial texture of the US.

The monetary progress of tobacco likewise added to the advancement of worldwide exchange organizations. Tobacco turned into an essential product in worldwide exchange, making financial conditions and molding strategic connections between countries. The three-sided shipping lanes that worked with the trading of tobacco, among different products, between the Americas, Europe, and Africa highlighted the interconnectedness of worldwide economies during this period.

The financial meaning of tobacco was not bound to the estates; it reached out to different subordinate businesses. Tobacco handling, assembling of smoking gear, and the ascent of tobacco vendors generally added to the enhancement of economies in locales where tobacco was developed and consumed. This financial enhancement, while encouraging flourishing in certain districts, likewise planted the seeds of monetary disparity and abuse.

The nineteenth century saw a change in outlook in tobacco utilization with the rise of the cigarette. This minimized and normalized type of tobacco utilization denoted a takeoff from the formal and relaxed nature of smoking lines and stogies. The cigarette, with its comfort and reasonableness, turned into the favored method of smoking, democratizing the propensity and making it open to a more extensive populace.

The ascent of the cigarette was joined by changes in smoking manners and standards. Smoking turned out to be more predominant out in the open spaces, from cafés to transportation, affecting the plan of public regions and social collaborations. Smoking turned into a fundamental piece of different social ceremonies, from after-supper stogies to the trading of cigarettes as a token of brotherhood.

Tobacco's unavoidable impact reached out past the actual demonstration of smoking to shape social articulations and creative portrayals. The commonness of smoking in writing, craftsmanship, and film verified its embeddedness in the social climate. Smoking turned into an image of complexity, defiance, and existential consideration in different creative developments, leaving a permanent engraving on social creation.

The mid-twentieth century denoted a defining moment in the cultural view of tobacco as logical examination progressively connected smoking to extreme wellbeing chances. The Top health spokesperson's Report in the US in 1964 was a turning point, formally recognizing the risks of smoking and provoking a change in open perspectives. This acknowledgment encouraged a progression of general wellbeing mediations, remembering smoking boycotts for public spaces, expanded tax collection on tobacco items, and rigid guidelines on tobacco promoting.

The changing impression of smoking affected cultural standards and ways of behaving. Smoking, once inseparable from excitement and cultural acknowledgment, became disparaged. The tobacco business confronted lawful difficulties, and hostile to smoking efforts tried to teach the general population about the wellbeing gambles related with tobacco use. The decrease in smoking rates in many created nations mirrored a basic change in cultural qualities, focusing on wellbeing and prosperity over the once-glitzy charm of tobacco.

The cultural changes going with the inescapable reception of tobacco enlighten the intricate transaction between culture, economy, and wellbeing. Tobacco, at first embraced for its curiosity and seen benefits, turned into a two sided deal, leaving a path of financial flourishing yet additionally wellbeing outcomes afterward. The tale of tobacco is one of social development and variation, monetary double-dealing, and, at last, a retribution with the wellbeing effects of a once-celebrated propensity.

The social, financial, and social changes prodded by tobacco's boundless reception highlight the diverse idea of cultural change. From the development of smoking as a shared movement that rose above friendly classes to the financial repercussions of tobacco development and exchange, the effect of tobacco on social orders is significant and broad. As we ponder these changes, it prompts us to think about the continuous strain between individual decisions and aggregate prosperity, the intricacies of social practices, and the basic to explore a way that adjusts custom with developing cultural qualities.

Proceeding with our investigation of the cultural changes going with the far reaching reception of tobacco, we dig further into the nuanced layers of its effect on human way of behaving, social designs, and general wellbeing.

The mid-twentieth century denoted a seismic change in the cultural impression of tobacco as logical proof connecting smoking to serious wellbeing gambles started to collect. The Top health spokesperson's Report in the US in 1964 was an essential second, unequivocally laying out the relationship among smoking and sicknesses like cellular breakdown in the lungs and coronary illness. This disclosure set off a change in perspective in open mentalities towards smoking, changing it from a socially OK propensity to a vilified conduct.

The freshly discovered consciousness of the wellbeing gambles related with smoking provoked a progression of general wellbeing intercessions pointed toward moderating the effect of tobacco on people and society at large. State run administrations overall executed smoking boycotts out in the open spaces, going from cafés and bars to public transportation. These limitations reshaped the social scene, modifying the elements of regular cooperations and testing the profoundly imbued standard of smoking in different group environments.

The execution of smoking boycotts not just pointed toward shielding non-smokers from the risks of handed-down cigarette smoke yet in addition looked to establish conditions that put smoking commencement and empowered end down. Without smoke strategies assumed a critical part in reshaping normal practices encompassing smoking, flagging an aggregate obligation to focus on general wellbeing over individual smoking privileges.

At the same time, tax collection on tobacco items was expanded as an obstacle to smoking. Greater costs planned to beat tobacco utilization down, particularly among more youthful populaces and lower-pay people. The financial component of smoking went through change as the expense of the propensity expanded, adding to a decrease in smoking rates over the long run.

The defamation of smoking likewise appeared in moving social discernments. Smoking, once viewed as impressive and modern, became related with wellbeing dangers, dependence, and cultural dismissal for prosperity. This social change was reflected in media portrayals, where smoking characters in movies and TV step by step dwindled, and smoking scenes confronted examination for expected effect on more youthful crowds.

The tobacco business, which had long blossomed with developing a picture of charm and refinement around smoking, confronted remarkable difficulties. Fights in court, legal claims, and severe guidelines shortened the business' capacity to glamorize and advance its items. Hostile to smoking efforts, frequently including realistic portrayals of the wellbeing outcomes of smoking, looked to neutralize many years of tobacco promoting and present an obvious rude awakening to potential and current smokers.

The switching social scene up smoking met with advancing orientation elements. While smoking had at first been related essentially with men, the rising acknowledgment of smoking among ladies during the ahead of schedule to mid-twentieth century was met with difficulties as wellbeing concerns acquired noticeable quality. The tobacco business, perceiving the undiscovered market among ladies, designated female purchasers with promoting that frequently spoke to thoughts of freedom and uniformity. Nonetheless, as the wellbeing chances turned out to be more evident, ladies' smoking rates additionally confronted examination, prompting shifts in orientation explicit promoting and designated end endeavors.

The decrease in smoking rates saw in many created nations over the last 50% of the twentieth 100 years and into the 21st century mirrors the summit of these multi-layered cultural changes. Wellbeing cognizance, informed by logical examination and general wellbeing efforts, acquired unmistakable quality, reshaping individual mentalities towards tobacco use. Smoking suspension projects and emotionally supportive networks turned out to be more common, helping the individuals who wished to break liberated from the habit-forming hold of tobacco.

The cultural changes going with the inescapable reception of tobacco highlight the intricate transaction between individual decisions, social standards, and general wellbeing objectives. The direction of tobacco use uncovers the pliability of cultural mentalities in light of developing information and changing social qualities. From the mutual ceremonies of native societies to the boundless reception of smoking across classes in Europe, to the resulting defamation and decrease in smoking rates, the excursion of tobacco is one of dynamic changes.

The difficulties presented by tobacco use are not restricted to individual wellbeing; they reach out to more extensive cultural contemplations. The monetary conditions based on tobacco development, the double-dealing implanted in its set of experiences, and the sweeping results of smoking on general wellbeing required an aggregate reaction. The cultural changes encompassing tobacco use epitomize the fragile harmony between individual opportunities, monetary interests, and the all-encompassing liability to defend public prosperity.

As we ponder the cultural changes going with the inescapable reception of tobacco, it prompts us to think about the continuous discourse between private decisions and aggregate wellbeing needs. The excursion of tobacco through social orders fills in as a demonstration of the limit of societies to adjust, develop, and face difficulties. It likewise features the obligation of social orders to tackle information, shape strategies, and cultivate conditions that focus on wellbeing and prosperity, guaranteeing a future where the effect of tobacco on people and networks is moderated and limited.

Chapter 3

The Science Behind Addiction

Investigating the many-sided scene of compulsion dives into the intricate exchange of science, brain research, and neurochemistry that underlies the convincing power of habit-forming ways of behaving. The science behind compulsion is a multi-layered embroidery, winding around together hereditary inclinations, brain transformations, and natural impacts. Understanding the systems that drive habit is essential for logical request as well as for creating successful methodologies for avoidance, treatment, and recuperation.

At the center of dependence lies the cerebrum, a surprising organ that coordinates the heap elements of the body and assumes a focal part in forming ways of behaving. The mind's prize framework, represented by an organization of synapses and receptors, is a central participant in the study of dependence. Dopamine, frequently alluded to as the "vibe great" synapse, becomes the overwhelming focus in the award framework, balancing joy, inspiration, and support.

The excursion into compulsion frequently starts with openness to substances or ways of behaving that initiate the cerebrum's award hardware. Whether it's medications, liquor, or exercises like betting or gaming, the underlying experience sets off the arrival of dopamine in key districts of the mind, making a feeling of joy and building up the relationship between the boost and the prize. This support lays out the establishment for the advancement of habit-forming designs.

Hereditary elements contribute altogether to a singular's defenselessness to habit. The heritability of habit has been broadly perceived, with various examinations featuring the job of hereditary varieties in impacting weakness. Explicit qualities engaged with synapse guideline, reward handling, and stress reaction can influence a singular's inclination to habit-forming ways of behaving. In any case, it's vital to take note of that hereditary qualities alone don't decide habit; ecological variables and individual decisions likewise assume significant parts.

Natural impacts, particularly during basic formative stages, shape the gamble of habit. Adolescence encounters, openness to injury, relational peculiarities, and financial elements can add to the weakness or flexibility of a person. Unfriendly youth encounters, specifically, have been connected to an improved probability of taking part in habit-forming ways of behaving sometime down the road. The transaction among nature and support, where hereditary inclinations cross with ecological triggers, shapes the background of habit powerlessness.

Brain adaptability, the mind's capacity to adjust and redesign itself in light of encounters, is a basic part of compulsion. Drawn out openness to drugs or ways of behaving prompts primary and useful changes in the cerebrum's prize hardware. This reworking can prompt an increased aversion to the substance or conduct, a peculiarity known as refinement. Alternately, resilience might create, requiring expanded measures of the substance or commitment to the way of behaving to accomplish a similar degree of remuneration.

The prefrontal cortex, a locale of the cerebrum liable for navigation, drive control, and judgment, assumes a urgent part in compulsion. Ongoing openness to habit-forming upgrades can impede the capability of the prefrontal cortex, decreasing its capacity to apply chief command over rash ways of behaving. This lopsidedness between the hasty drive for sure fire reward and the reduced limit with respect to poise adds to the propagation of habit-forming cycles.

The mesolimbic dopamine framework, associating the ventral tegmental region (VTA) to the core accumbens, is a focal pathway in the cerebrum's prize hardware. The arrival of dopamine in the core accumbens supports ways of behaving related with joy and award. Medications of misuse, like cocaine or narcotics, frequently apply their belongings by capturing this normal prize framework. The flood of dopamine delivered by these substances overpowers the mind's ordinary administrative systems, making a fake and extraordinary feeling of joy.

Substances that instigate critical dopamine delivery can make a strong relationship between the medication and prize, encouraging a habitual drive to search out the substance notwithstanding unfortunate results. This shift from intentional medication use to impulsive medication looking for is a sign of habit. The progress from sporting use to dependence includes neurochemical changes as well as modifications in the examples of quality articulation and neuronal availability.

The idea of the "reward lack disorder" sets that people with specific hereditary variations might have a lessened reaction to normal prizes, inclining them toward search out substances or ways of behaving that misleadingly help dopamine levels. This lack in the cerebrum's prize framework can add to an elevated weakness to compulsion. The comprehension of remuneration lack has suggestions for customized ways to deal with dependence treatment, taking into account individual varieties in hereditary cosmetics.

Ongoing openness to drugs prompts a peculiarity known as resistance, where the individual requires expanding measures of the substance to accomplish a similar degree of remuneration. Resistance is firmly connected to neuroadaptations in the cerebrum's award hardware, remembering changes for receptor awareness and synapse discharge. This heightening resistance adds to the pattern of compulsion, driving people to raise their substance use in quest for the decreasing prizes.

Withdrawal side effects, the physiological and mental impacts that happen when substance use is stopped, further muddle the habit-forming cycle. The mind, having adjusted to the presence of the substance, responds to its evacuation with a scope of side effects. These side effects can incorporate nervousness, crabbiness, sorrow, and profound desires, driving people to look for alleviation through proceeded with substance use. The evasion of withdrawal side effects turns into a strong inspiration for keeping up with habit-forming ways of behaving.

The supporting impacts of drugs are not restricted to the prompt joy got from their utilization. The memory of the pleasurable experience, combined with ecological signals related with substance use, can set off strong desires even after times of forbearance. This acquainted growing experience adds to the steadiness of fixation and the high gamble of backslide, even after fruitful treatment mediations.

The study of fixation stretches out past substance maltreatment to incorporate conduct addictions, like betting or gaming problems. While the particular ways of behaving and brain systems might vary, the center standards of remuneration, support, and brain adaptability stay focal. Social addictions actuate comparative mind circuits engaged with handling rewards, making enthusiastic examples of conduct driven by the quest for joy.

Understanding the neurobiological underpinnings of habit has significant ramifications for the improvement of successful avoidance and treatment systems. Avoidance endeavors can be educated by bits of knowledge into the hereditary and natural factors that add to weakness. Early mediations, particularly for people with realized risk factors, can assist with alleviating the effect of antagonistic encounters and decrease the probability of creating habit-forming ways of behaving.

Treatment approaches for habit influence the pliancy of the mind to advance recuperation. Conduct treatments, like mental social treatment (CBT) and possibility the executives, plan to reshape maladaptive thought processes and conduct. Prescriptions, like methadone or buprenorphine for narcotic enslavement, can assist with overseeing withdrawal side effects and lessen desires, working with the course of recuperation.

The arising area of neuropharmacology offers new roads for designated mediations. Meds that adjust explicit synapse frameworks, for example, dopamine or glutamate, show guarantee in assisting people with beating the difficulties of enslavement. The advancement of customized treatment plans, considering individual hereditary varieties, holds the possibility to upgrade the viability of intercessions and work on long haul results.

The science behind fixation isn't exclusively centered around the singular level; it additionally thinks about the more extensive cultural setting. Social determinants, including monetary incongruities, admittance to medical services, and local area support, impact both the gamble of fixation and the open doors for recuperation. Thorough ways to deal with habit should address the neurobiological angles as well as the social, financial, and social factors that add to the pervasiveness and steadiness of habit-forming ways of behaving.

Examination into the study of habit is continuous, uncovering new bits of knowledge into the atomic and brain instruments that drive impulsive ways of behaving. Progresses in neuroimaging, hereditary qualities, and pharmacology keep on refining how we might interpret habit, making ready for additional designated and viable mediations. As we unwind the intricacies of enslavement at the sub-atomic and cell levels, the reconciliation of this information into all encompassing, patient-focused approaches holds the commitment of changing the scene of fixation treatment and recuperation.

3.1 Dive into the chemistry of tobacco and the addictive properties of nicotine.

Jumping into the science of tobacco uncovers a mind boggling mixture of mixtures, with nicotine standing apart as the essential psychoactive fixing liable for the habit-forming properties of tobacco items.

Understanding the perplexing collaborations between the synthetic compounds in tobacco and the human body reveals insight into the components basic nicotine compulsion, a basic viewpoint in tending to the difficulties of tobacco reliance.

Tobacco, got from the Nicotiana class of plants, includes various species, with Nicotiana tabacum and Nicotiana rustica being the most broadly developed for business use. The leaves of these plants contain a horde of synthetic compounds, yet nicotine becomes the dominant focal point as the main alkaloid liable for the habit-forming nature of tobacco.

Nicotine, a normally happening alkaloid, has a place with the class of mixtures known as alkaloids, which are natural particles containing nitrogen. Fundamentally, nicotine bears similarity to synapses like acetylcholine, permitting it to interface with and impact the capability of the sensory system. The compound recipe of nicotine is C10H14N2, mirroring its sythesis of carbon, hydrogen, and nitrogen particles.

The course of enslavement starts with the inward breath of nicotine-containing tobacco smoke or the ingestion of nicotine through different means, like smokeless tobacco items. At the point when tobacco is copied, as on account of smoking, a perplexing cluster of synthetics is delivered as smoke. This smoke is a heterogeneous combination including gases, spray particles, and disintegrated compounds, each adding to the generally tangible experience of smoking.

The burning of tobacco produces a plenty of substance compounds, some of which are exceptionally harmful. Among the a great many synthetic compounds distinguished in tobacco smoke, a few are perceived cancer-causing agents and supporters of different respiratory sicknesses. Models incorporate tar, benzene, formaldehyde, and polycyclic sweet-smelling hydrocarbons. The unsafe impacts of these mixtures highlight the wellbeing gambles related with smoking past nicotine compulsion.

Nicotine, regardless of being the habit-forming part, isn't the essential supporter of the unfavorable wellbeing impacts related with tobacco use. All things being equal, it is different constituents of tobacco smoke that present critical wellbeing gambles. Notwithstanding, nicotine's strong habit-forming properties drive the proceeded with utilization of tobacco items, putting forth it a basic concentration in attempts to address tobacco reliance.

At the point when tobacco is smoked, nicotine is quickly retained through the lungs and enters the circulation system. From that point, it crosses the blood-mind obstruction, a semi-penetrable layer that isolates the circulatory system from the cerebrum. Once in the cerebrum, nicotine collaborates with a class of receptors known as nicotinic acetylcholine receptors (nAChRs), copying the impacts of acetylcholine, a synapse engaged with different physiological cycles.

The initiation of nAChRs by nicotine prompts the arrival of synapses, including dopamine, serotonin, and norepinephrine. Dopamine, specifically, assumes a focal part in the mind's prize framework, adding to the pleasurable sensations related with nicotine utilization. The arrival of dopamine in key mind locales, for example, the core accumbens, supports the relationship among smoking and prize, making a strong motivation to rehash the way of behaving.

The supporting impacts of nicotine stretch out past the quick joy experienced during smoking. The cerebrum's prize framework goes through transformations because of ongoing nicotine openness, adding to the advancement of resistance and reliance. Resilience alludes to the peculiarity where an individual requires expanding measures of nicotine to accomplish a similar degree of delight, while reliance appears as the dependence on nicotine to keep away from withdrawal side effects.

Nicotine withdrawal is a critical consider the support of tobacco reliance. At the point when nicotine levels in the body decline, people might encounter a scope of physical and mental side effects, including peevishness, tension, discouraged state of mind, and profound desires for nicotine. The evasion of withdrawal side effects turns into a strong inspiration for proceeded with tobacco use, propagating the habit-forming cycle.

The building up impacts of nicotine are not restricted to the focal sensory system; they additionally reach out to fringe tissues. Nicotine impacts different physiological cycles, including pulse, circulatory strain, and gastrointestinal capability. These fringe impacts add to the general insight of smoking and further build up the ongoing idea of tobacco use.

The pharmacokinetics of nicotine, including its retention, appropriation, digestion, and end, impact its habit-forming potential. The course of organization altogether influences the speed and force of nicotine's belongings. Inward breath of tobacco smoke gives a fast and proficient course for nicotine retention, prompting a speedy beginning of compensating impacts. Smokeless tobacco items, like biting tobacco or snuff, likewise convey nicotine however at a more slow rate contrasted with smoking.

Nicotine goes through digestion essentially in the liver, where it is separated into different metabolites, including cotinine. Cotinine is a significant metabolite of nicotine and fills in as a biomarker for tobacco openness in research and clinical settings. The disposal half-existence of nicotine shifts among people however is for the most part generally short, adding to the continuous utilization of tobacco items to keep up with reliable nicotine levels.

The hereditary fluctuation in the digestion of nicotine adds to individual contrasts in the reaction to tobacco. Catalysts engaged with nicotine digestion, like cytochrome P450 2A6 (CYP2A6), show hereditary polymorphisms that impact the rate at which nicotine is used. People with specific hereditary variations might encounter either a more slow or quicker digestion of nicotine, influencing their helplessness to tobacco reliance.

Past the pharmacological activities of nicotine, the ceremonial and tangible parts of smoking assume an essential part in tobacco enslavement. The demonstration of smoking becomes imbued in everyday schedules and social cooperations, making relationship between ecological prompts and the remunerating impacts of nicotine. The smell, taste, and material sensations related with smoking add to the social and mental parts of habit.

Tending to tobacco reliance includes a complete methodology that thinks about both the pharmacological and conduct parts of compulsion. Nicotine substitution treatments (NRTs, for example, nicotine patches, gum, capsules, nasal showers, and inhalers, give a controlled and steadily diminishing portion of nicotine to assist people with overseeing withdrawal side effects during the stopping system. NRTs mean to decouple the supporting impacts of nicotine from the hurtful parts of tobacco smoke, working with a progress to forbearance.

Different drugs, like bupropion and varenicline, target explicit synapse frameworks to lessen desires and withdrawal side effects. Bupropion, initially created as an energizer, has been found to help smoking discontinuance by regulating dopamine and norepinephrine levels in the mind. Varenicline, an incomplete agonist of nAChRs, acts by both invigorating and hindering the receptors, lessening the pleasurable impacts of nicotine and relieving withdrawal side effects.

Social intercessions, including mental conduct treatment (CBT) and persuasive talking, address the mental parts of tobacco reliance. These methodologies assist people with recognizing triggers for smoking, foster survival techniques, and fabricate flexibility against backslide. Support gatherings and directing administrations assume a pivotal part in furnishing people with the devices and backing expected to explore the difficulties of stopping.

General wellbeing drives pointed toward forestalling tobacco use and advancing end likewise assume a crucial part in tending to the more extensive cultural effect of tobacco compulsion. Hostile to smoking efforts, limitations on tobacco promoting, and the execution of without smoke strategies add to changing accepted practices and decreasing the predominance of smoking. Training and mindfulness programs target the two people and networks, encouraging a climate that deters tobacco use and supports those trying to stop.

The study of tobacco enslavement ceaselessly develops as scientists uncover new experiences into the atomic and brain components included. Propels in neuroscience, hereditary qualities, and pharmacology give an establishment to the improvement of imaginative mediations and customized treatment draws near. The continuous journey to unwind the intricacies of nicotine habit holds the commitment of further developing results for people wrestling with tobacco reliance and diminishing the worldwide weight of tobacco-related infections.

3.2 Discuss the psychological and physiological effects of smoking on the human body.

Talking about the mental and physiological impacts of smoking on the human body requires an investigation of the unpredictable transaction between the compound parts of tobacco smoke and the intricate frameworks of the body. From the quick effect on the respiratory and cardiovascular frameworks to the drawn out results on emotional wellness and generally speaking prosperity, smoking applies a complex impact with broad ramifications.

Prompt Physiological Impacts:

Respiratory Framework:

The inward breath of tobacco smoke uncovered the respiratory framework to a strong combination of synthetic compounds, prompting quick and significant impacts. Aggravations like tar, formaldehyde, and acrolein can arouse the aviation routes and weaken the capability of cilia, small hair-like designs that assist with cleaning bodily fluid and garbage off of the lungs. This disturbance adds to the trademark hack found in smokers.

Nicotine, the habit-forming part of tobacco, chokes veins and increments pulse, prompting an ascent in circulatory strain. The bronchioles, little air entries in the lungs, additionally contract, making it harder to relax. These intense impacts add to the feeling of readiness and expanded energy frequently experienced by smokers.

Carbon monoxide, a harmful gas present in tobacco smoke, contends with oxygen for restricting to hemoglobin in red platelets. This decreases the blood's ability to convey oxygen, prompting a condition of hypoxia (oxygen hardship) in different tissues.

Cardiovascular Framework:

The cardiovascular framework bears the prompt brunt of smoking's effect. Nicotine invigorates the arrival of adrenaline, a chemical that increments pulse and circulatory strain. At the same time, carbon monoxide lessens how much oxygen that can be moved by the blood. These consolidated impacts hoist the gamble of respiratory failures and strokes, especially in people with prior cardiovascular circumstances.

Focal Sensory system:

Nicotine's fast retention into the circulatory system works with its excursion to the cerebrum, where it animates the arrival of synapses like dopamine. This flood in dopamine levels adds to the pleasurable sensations related with smoking. All the while, nicotine enacts the thoughtful sensory system, prompting expanded readiness and a feeling of unwinding.

Long haul Physiological Impacts:

Respiratory Framework:

Constant openness to tobacco smoke is a significant gamble factor for respiratory infections, including ongoing obstructive pneumonic illness (COPD), emphysema, and persistent bronchitis. The aggregate harm to the lung tissue impedes its capacity to effectively work. The continuous irritation and oxidative pressure add to the movement of these circumstances, prompting a decrease in lung capability over the long run.

The gamble of cellular breakdown in the lungs, one of the deadliest outcomes of smoking, is altogether raised. Cancer-causing intensifies in tobacco smoke, for example, polycyclic fragrant hydrocarbons and nitrosamines, harm the DNA in lung cells, making ready for the uncontrolled development of carcinogenic cells.

Cardiovascular Framework:

Smoking affects the cardiovascular framework. Ongoing openness to nicotine adds to the advancement of atherosclerosis, the limiting and solidifying of supply routes because of the development of plaque. This interaction expands the gamble of coronary course illness, fringe vein infection, and other vascular inconveniences.

The elevated pulse coming about because of smoking overwhelms the heart, improving the probability of coronary episodes and other cardiovascular occasions. The mix of atherosclerosis and expanded coagulating hazard can prompt the development of blood clumps, further compromising blood stream to crucial organs.

People who smoke over a lengthy period face a raised gamble of creating cardiovascular infections, including cardiovascular breakdown and arrhythmias. The combined harm to the supply routes and the heart's underlying changes add to these drawn out results.

Stomach related Framework:

Smoking influences the stomach related framework, expanding the gamble of peptic ulcers and gastrointestinal reflux. The harmful parts in tobacco smoke, like nicotine and hydrochloric corrosive, can debilitate the lower esophageal sphincter, permitting stomach corrosive to stream once again into the throat. This adds to the improvement of conditions like gastroesophageal reflux sickness (GERD).

Furthermore, smoking is a huge gamble factor for pancreatic disease. The cancer-causing agents in tobacco smoke might add to the hereditary changes that lead to the uncontrolled development of pancreatic cells.

Conceptive Framework:

Smoking unfavorably affects the regenerative framework in all kinds of people. In ladies, smoking can affect fruitfulness and increment the gamble of entanglements during pregnancy, including preterm birth, low birth weight, and stillbirth. The poisonous substances in tobacco smoke can likewise influence the creating hatchling, prompting long haul medical problems for the youngster.

In men, smoking is related with erectile brokenness. The tightening of veins and disability of blood stream, the two results of smoking, add to troubles in accomplishing and keeping an erection.

Mental Impacts:

Habit and Reliance:

Nicotine, the essential psychoactive compound in tobacco, is profoundly habit-forming. It follows up on the cerebrum's prize framework, making a pattern of encouraging feedback that cultivates reliance. The quick arrival of dopamine in light of nicotine adds to the pleasurable sensations and the craving to rehash the way of behaving.

Reliance on nicotine can appear as desires, peevishness, nervousness, and trouble concentrating while endeavoring to stop or eliminate smoking. The supporting impacts of nicotine on the cerebrum's prize pathways make breaking the pattern of dependence a critical test for some smokers.

State of mind and Emotional well-being:

While numerous people go to smoking for apparent pressure alleviation or unwinding, the drawn out influence on psychological well-being is unfavorable. Smoking has been connected to an expanded gamble of tension and misery. The specific components behind this affiliation are complicated, including both the immediate impacts of nicotine on synapse frameworks and the more extensive psychosocial setting in which smoking happens.

People with mental circumstances, like schizophrenia, are bound to smoke, and smoking rates are excessively high among people with psychological well-being issues. Oneself sedating speculation sets that people with emotional wellness issues might involve smoking as a survival strategy to ease side effects.

Mental Capability:

Smoking has been displayed to adversely affect mental capability and is related with an expanded gamble of mental degradation and dementia in more seasoned age. The diminished blood stream to the mind, oxidative pressure, and aggravation initiated by smoking add to these mental impedances.

In addition, smoking during pre-adulthood has been connected to changes in mind design and capability, influencing regions associated with drive control, direction, and award handling. This highlights the significance of avoidance endeavors focusing on youth to moderate the drawn out mental results of smoking.

Handed-down cigarette smoke:

The unsafe impacts of smoking are not restricted to the smoker; handed-down cigarette smoke presents huge dangers to those uncovered. Handed-down cigarette smoke, otherwise called latent smoke or natural tobacco smoke, contains large numbers of similar poisonous and cancer-causing compounds as straightforwardly breathed in smoke.

Respiratory Impacts:

Handed-down cigarette smoke openness is especially destructive to kids, as their creating respiratory frameworks are more powerless. Kids presented to handed-down cigarette smoke are at an expanded gamble of respiratory diseases, asthma, and abrupt newborn child demise disorder (SIDS). Pregnant ladies presented to handed-down cigarette smoke face a raised gamble of inconveniences, including low birth weight and pre-term birth.

Cardiovascular Impacts:

The cardiovascular results of handed-down cigarette smoke openness reflect those found in dynamic smokers. Non-smokers presented to handed-down cigarette smoke might encounter an expanded gamble of coronary illness, stroke, and other cardiovascular circumstances. The hurtful impacts reach out to the two kids and grown-ups, stressing the significance of establishing without smoke conditions to safeguard general wellbeing.

Stopping and Recuperation:

While the physiological and mental impacts of smoking cast a considerable shadow, stopping smoking yields quick and long haul medical advantages. The body has a noteworthy limit with regards to mending, and the choice to stop smoking is one of the most significant stages toward further developing wellbeing and prosperity.

Quick Advantages:

Worked on Respiratory Capability: Promptly after stopping, the respiratory framework starts to recuperate. Cilia begin recovering, working with the getting free from bodily fluid and garbage from the lungs.

Upgraded Course: Nicotine's vasoconstrictive impacts lessen, prompting further developed blood stream and a decrease in circulatory strain.

Diminished Carbon Monoxide Levels: The end of smoking prompts a fast decrease in carbon monoxide levels in the blood, reestablishing its oxygen-conveying limit.

Long haul Advantages:

Diminished Chance of Sickness: The gamble of coronary illness, stroke, respiratory infections, and different diseases diminishes after some time.

The more drawn out a singular remaining parts without smoke, the more prominent the decrease in these dangers.

Worked on Psychological wellness: Stopping smoking has been related with upgrades in temperament, diminished nervousness, and a decreased gamble of sorrow. The emotional wellness benefits stretch out to both quick and long haul recuperation.

Upgraded Personal satisfaction: Smoking end brings about a general improvement in personal satisfaction, with expanded energy, better actual wellness, and a feeling of achievement.

Difficulties and Backing:

Withdrawal Side effects: Stopping smoking can be trying because of withdrawal side effects like desires, touchiness, and trouble concentrating. Nicotine substitution treatments (NRTs), drugs, and social mediations can offer help during the stopping system.

Conduct Methodologies: Taking on social procedures, for example, distinguishing triggers for smoking and creating ways of dealing with hardship or stress, is critical for long haul achievement. Support gatherings, guiding, and customized quit plans add to an extensive way to deal with stopping.

The Complicated Nexus of Mental and Physiological Impacts:

The complicated exchange between the mental and physiological impacts of smoking on the human body makes a perplexing nexus that shapes the experience of smokers and highlights the difficulties of tobacco fixation.

Mental Impacts:

Stress and Survival techniques:

Smoking is many times seen as a pressure help system, with people going to cigarettes in snapshots of strain or tension. Be that as it may, the evident pressure decrease is underhanded, as smoking eventually compounds pressure over the long haul.

The pattern of nicotine reliance makes a dependence on smoking as a method for dealing with especially difficult times, supporting the relationship among stress and the demonstration of smoking.

Social treatments pointed toward recognizing elective survival methods assume an essential part in breaking this cycle. Creating better ways of overseeing pressure, like activity, care, or social help, assists people with exploring difficulties without depending on smoking.

Dependence and Desires:

Nicotine's strong habit-forming properties make a strong pattern of reliance, where desires for nicotine become imbued in everyday schedules and exercises. The mental impulse to smoke is interwoven with the physiological requirement for nicotine, framing a building up circle that can be trying to break.

Mental social treatments (CBT) and pharmacological intercessions address the mental parts of dependence. CBT helps people recognize and challenge the contemplations and ways of behaving that add to smoking, while drugs like nicotine substitution treatments (NRTs) or physician endorsed prescriptions help with overseeing desires.

Social and Conduct Impacts:

Smoking is much of the time affected by friendly and ecological elements, with the demonstration of smoking profoundly implanted in friendly ceremonies and collaborations. The mental effect of social impacts can add to the trouble of stopping, as people might connect smoking with explicit settings, exercises, or groups of friends.

Extensive smoking suspension programs perceive the significance of tending to these social and conduct angles. Support gatherings, guiding administrations, and local area based drives add to establishing conditions that energize stopping and give an organization of help.

Physiological Impacts:

Lung Wellbeing and Respiratory Effect:

The physiological results of smoking on the respiratory framework are significant and complex. Constant openness to tobacco smoke prompts the amassing of tar in the lungs, causing irritation, limiting of aviation routes, and irreversible harm to lung tissue. The gamble of persistent respiratory circumstances, including constant obstructive aspiratory illness (COPD), raises with delayed smoking.

Smoking suspension is a urgent move toward moderating these respiratory impacts. The body's striking limit with regards to recuperating is obvious as lung capability improves, irritation diminishes, and the gamble of respiratory contaminations decreases subsequent to stopping.

Cardiovascular Results:

The effect of smoking on the cardiovascular framework stretches out past quick impacts to long haul results. Atherosclerosis, portrayed by the development of plaque in veins, expands the gamble of cardiovascular failures, strokes, and fringe vascular illnesses. Nicotine's impact on pulse and pulse puts extra weight on the cardiovascular framework.

Stopping smoking starts a positive fountain of changes in the cardiovascular framework. Circulatory strain diminishes, pulse standardizes, and the gamble of cardiovascular occasions decreases, underscoring the significance of smoking discontinuance as a cardiovascular gamble decrease system.

Disease Hazard and Cell Harm:

The cancer-causing intensifies in tobacco smoke add to the improvement of different tumors, with cellular breakdown in the lungs being the most conspicuous. Smoking is additionally connected to tumors of the mouth, throat, throat, pancreas, bladder, and that's only the tip of the iceberg. The cycle includes DNA harm, hereditary transformations, and the uncontrolled development of strange cells.

Smoking end is the best preventive measure against tobacco-related diseases. The decrease in openness to cancer-causing agents permits the body to start fix processes, lessening the gamble of cell changes and disease improvement.

Regenerative Wellbeing Suggestions:

Smoking applies tremendous consequences for conceptive wellbeing, affecting fruitfulness and pregnancy results. In ladies, smoking is related with troubles in considering, expanded chance of unsuccessful labor, pre-term birth, and low birth weight. In men, smoking has been connected to erectile brokenness and diminished sperm quality.

The positive effect of stopping smoking on regenerative wellbeing is clear in superior fruitfulness rates, better pregnancies, and improved results for the two moms and newborn children.

All encompassing Ways to deal with Smoking End:

Tending to the complicated trap of mental and physiological impacts of smoking requires comprehensive methodologies that recognize the interconnectedness of psyche and body.

Extensive Help Projects:

Viable smoking end programs envelop a scope of mediations, including conduct treatments, guiding, pharmacological help, and local area based drives. These projects perceive the significance of tending to both the mental reliance on smoking and the physiological outcomes.

Training and Anticipation:

General wellbeing endeavors assume an essential part in forestalling smoking commencement and advancing consciousness of the wellbeing gambles related with tobacco use. Instructive missions focusing on youth, guardians, and networks add to establishing conditions that put smoking down.

Strategy and Natural Changes:

Without smoke arrangements, limitations on tobacco publicizing, and tax assessment on tobacco items are basic parts of complete tobacco control methodologies. These actions diminish openness to handed-down cigarette smoke as well as establish conditions that help people in their endeavors to stop smoking.

Customized Treatment Plans:

Perceiving the singular varieties in smoking examples, inspirations, and wellbeing contemplations, customized treatment plans upgrade the adequacy of smoking suspension endeavors. Customized mediations, taking into account factors like hereditary qualities, psychological wellness, and social impacts, add to additional effective results.

Taking everything into account, the conversation of the mental and physiological impacts of smoking on the human body enlightens the complex and entwined nature of tobacco dependence. The affirmation of this intricacy highlights the significance of diverse ways to deal with smoking suspension that address both the mental and physiological components of the test. By coordinating social mediations, emotionally supportive networks, and general wellbeing drives, people can leave on an excursion toward better wellbeing and prosperity, liberated from the hold of tobacco compulsion.

The conversation of the mental and physiological impacts of smoking on the human body highlights the significant effect of this complicated way of behaving. From the quick physiological reactions to the drawn out results on respiratory and cardiovascular wellbeing, smoking pervades each feature of the body's perplexing frameworks. All the while, the mental impacts, incorporating dependence, temperament balance, and mental impacts, uncover the many-sided exchange among nicotine and the mind's award and administrative systems.

Tending to the difficulties presented by smoking includes a diverse methodology, enveloping counteraction, mediation, and backing for those trying to stop. General wellbeing drives focusing on the two smokers and nonsmokers add to a more extensive work to lessen the commonness of smoking and safeguard people from the unsafe impacts of tobacco.

Perceiving the strength of the human body and the potential for recuperation highlights the significance of smoking discontinuance as a groundbreaking move toward further developed wellbeing and prosperity.

Chapter 4

Tobacco Industry Tactics

The tobacco business, known for its verifiable and tenacious endeavors to advance, market, and sell tobacco items, has utilized a wide cluster of strategies notwithstanding the deeply grounded wellbeing chances related with smoking. These methodologies, going from forceful promoting and campaigning to designated publicizing and item development, highlight the business' versatility in keeping up with its piece of the pie and world-wide impact. A complete comprehension of these strategies is urgent for policymakers, general wellbeing advocates, and the overall population to foster viable countermeasures and protect general wellbeing.

One of the essential strategies utilized by the tobacco business is force-ful showcasing and promoting. Designated showcasing has been a long-standing methodology, with the business explicitly fitting its endeavors to engage different segment gatherings. Youth, ladies, and minority net-works have been specific targets, and the business has utilized seasoned cigarettes and outwardly engaging bundling to allure new, frequently un-derage, smokers. This has prompted administrative measures, including flavor boycotts and realistic admonition names, pointed toward checking youth commencement.

Sponsorship and advancement of occasions have additionally been normal strategies utilized by the tobacco business to connect its brands with positive and fabulous pictures. By supporting games, shows, and social celebrations, tobacco organizations make memorability and add to the standardization of smoking. While there have been expanding limi-tations on tobacco publicizing in numerous nations, these endeavors endure, adjusting to developing advertising scenes.

Retail location promoting addresses one more basic part of the busi-ness' methodology. Weighty interests in this space are settled on to impact buying choices. Item shows, special limits, and vital arrangement of tobacco items close to sales registers are strategies pointed toward expanding perceivability and driving deals. Endeavors to limit retail location showcasing have become fundamental in countering the business' impact at the retail level.

With the ascent of the web and virtual entertainment, the tobacco business has adjusted its advertising methodologies to online stages. Powerhouse showcasing, supported content, and intelligent missions are currently used to contact a wide crowd. This shift requests stricter guidelines on internet publicizing and advancement to address the business' developing strategies and forestall the evasion of customary promoting limitations.

As well as advertising, the tobacco business has been effectively engaged with campaigning and political impact to safeguard its inclinations. Political commitments, both immediate and roundabout, have been instrumental in forming regulation and guidelines connected with tobacco. By supporting up-and-comers thoughtful to the business' plan, adding to political activity councils, and participating in direct campaigning, tobacco organizations look to impact approaches in support of themselves.

Resistance to tobacco control strategies is a predictable subject in the business' endeavors. Measures, for example, charge increments, realistic admonition marks, and limitations on smoking out in the open spots have confronted steadfast opposition. The business frequently contends against these arrangements by stressing potential employment misfortunes, monetary effect, and individual opportunities. Such resistance features the requirement for carefulness in making and carrying out successful tobacco control measures.

The tobacco business has likewise tried to frame coalitions with outsider associations to enhance its impact and present a unified front against tobacco control strategies. These collusions, frequently framed with organizations, exchange affiliations, and front gatherings, give a stage to the business to push its plan. The impact of such partnerships can block the advancement of general wellbeing arrangements and highlights the significance of tending to industry impedance at numerous levels.

As far as item development and market extension, the tobacco business ceaselessly acquaints new items with keep up with piece of the pie and appeal to various shopper inclinations. Smokeless tobacco, e-cigarettes, and warmed tobacco items are instances of such developments. Advertised as less destructive other options, these items have started banters about their security, requesting continuous investigation and administrative reactions.

Additionally, the business has moved its concentration to developing business sectors where tobaco utilization is rising. Forceful showcasing efforts and careless guidelines in these locales add to expanded smoking rates, especially among weak populaces. This geological shift accentuates the requirement for worldwide participation to address the worldwide effect of tobacco industry strategies.

The tobacco business has tried to shape administrative systems for its potential benefit. This includes pushing for industry-accommodating guidelines, taking part in administrative cycles, and affecting worldwide economic deals. By using economic deals, the business can challenge and sabotage tobacco control measures, involving financial backer state debate settlement instruments to look for remuneration for saw misfortunes because of general wellbeing guidelines.

Defaming logical proof has been one more strategy utilized by the tobacco business. Financing problematic exploration to stir up misgivings about laid out logical connections among smoking and wellbeing chances, the business participates in what is known as the "vendor of uncertainty" methodology. By making disarray and discussion around the wellbeing effect of tobacco use, the business plans to subvert public trust in logical agreement.

Advertising efforts assume a part in controlling public discernment. Making light of the wellbeing dangers of smoking and moving fault to individual obligation are repeating subjects. Stressing individual decision and depicting smokers as dissidents or nonconformists can add to a positive public picture, regardless of the damages brought about by smoking. These missions have suggestions for public comprehension and backing for tobacco control strategies.

Preventing the habit-forming nature from getting nicotine has been a longstanding strategy of the tobacco business. Questioning the habit-forming properties of their items and, at times, advancing the possibility that stopping is simple, the business adds to an absence of public mindfulness about the difficulties of smoking suspension. This disavowal has thwarted endeavors to successfully address nicotine enslavement.

In fights in court, the tobacco business has reliably battled against guidelines. Difficulties to cautioning names, promoting limitations, and plain bundling prerequisites are normal. While the business has gotten a few lawful triumphs, administrative organizations and general wellbeing advocates have likewise prevailed with regards to executing measures to check tobacco industry impact.

Using corporate social obligation (CSR) drives, tobacco organizations participate in exercises to work on their public picture. This incorporates greenwashing and charity endeavors, for example, supporting local area projects, natural drives, or wellbeing programs. Pundits contend that such exercises are endeavors to occupy from the damages brought about by the business and to introduce a façade of social obligation.

Industry-upheld youth anticipation programs have been supported by tobacco organizations, raising worries about irreconcilable circumstances. By introducing themselves as accomplices in tending to youth smoking, the business might expect to impact the account around its part in advancing tobacco use. Such projects require examination to guarantee they don't think twice about respectability of veritable youth avoidance endeavors.

Taking everything into account, the tobacco business' strategies are assorted, versatile, and persevering. Regardless of huge advancement in tobacco control, the business keeps on tracking down ways of advancing its items, extend its market, and impact popular assessment and strategy. Compelling countermeasures include a multi-pronged methodology, including severe guidelines, public mindfulness missions, and worldwide participation. Fortifying administrative systems, lessening the business' impact on policymaking, and uncovering tricky promoting rehearses are fundamental stages toward accomplishing a without tobacco future. As the tobacco scene develops with the presentation of new items, administrative organizations and general wellbeing advocates should stay cautious to address arising difficulties and safeguard worldwide wellbeing.

4.1 Investigate the strategies employed by the tobacco industry in marketing and advertising.

Examining the procedures utilized by the tobacco business in promoting and publicizing uncovers a perplexing and modern scene molded by many years of developing strategies. The business' endeavors have been set apart by a tenacious quest for new business sectors, target socio-economics, and creative limited time procedures. Understanding these methodologies is critical for creating successful tobacco control strategies, safeguarding weak populaces, and battling the business' impact on open insight.

Designated Promoting:

One of the getting through techniques utilized by the tobacco business is designated showcasing, meaning to arrive at explicit segment bunches with custom-made messages and items. By and large, youth, ladies, and minority networks have been central marks of these endeavors.

The business perceives the possibility to lay out brand dedication from the get-go throughout everyday life, and advertising efforts frequently use subjects and symbolism that resound with more youthful crowds. The presentation of seasoned cigarettes, beautiful bundling, and limited time occasions explicitly focusing on youth has raised critical worries about the business' effect on underage smoking inception.

On account of ladies, tobacco organizations have utilized modern systems to connect smoking with ideas of freedom, strengthening, and marvelousness. Cigarette brands were promoted as accomplices to the advanced, freed lady, encouraging a picture of refinement. Additionally, crusades focusing on minority networks have utilized socially unambiguous subjects and symbolism, adding to differences in smoking pervasiveness. The treacherous idea of designated advertising requires cautiousness in observing and managing special exercises to safeguard weak populaces.

Sponsorship and Advancement:

The tobacco business has a background marked by supporting occasions and exercises for of advancing its brands and connecting them with positive and exciting pictures. By putting resources into games, shows, social celebrations, and other high-profile events, tobacco organizations intend to make positive relationship with their items. This strategy adds to the standardization of smoking and keeps up with brand perceivability in a jam-packed market.

Sports sponsorships have been especially conspicuous, with tobacco organizations adjusting their brands to well known athletic occasions. This affiliation makes an inner mind interface between actual wellness and smoking, in spite of the deeply grounded wellbeing chances. Show sponsorships and social celebrations give extra roads to the business to contact different crowds and implant its items in the texture of social encounters.

In spite of expanding limitations on tobacco promoting and sponsorship in numerous nations, the business keeps on tracking down creative ways of keeping a presence in the open arena. This determination highlights the requirement for exhaustive guidelines that reach out past conventional publicizing channels.

Retail location Advertising:

Retail location showcasing is a basic part of the tobacco business' procedure to impact buying choices. In retail conditions, tobacco organizations put vigorously in making outwardly engaging showcases, offering limited time limits, and decisively setting items close to sales registers. These endeavors mean to build the perceivability of tobacco items and benefit from drive buys.

Item shows at the retail location are painstakingly intended to stand out and make a positive picture around smoking. Special limits, for example, get one-get without one offers, are utilized to boost mass buys. Setting tobacco items close to sales registers ensures that they stay top-of-mind for shoppers during the checkout cycle.

Confining retail location promoting is a vital stage in controling the business' impact at the retail level. Guidelines that limit the perceivability of tobacco items and preclude specific special strategies add to establishing a climate that is less helpful for motivation buys and inception among non-smokers.

On the web and Virtual Entertainment Advancement:

With the approach of the web and online entertainment, the tobacco business has adjusted its promoting systems to these new stages. Online advancement incorporates a scope of exercises, from supported content on sites to drawing in with crowds via virtual entertainment stages. Powerhouse showcasing, where well known people elevate tobacco brands to their devotees, has turned into an unmistakable strategy.

Web-based entertainment stages give an immediate channel to contact a wide and various crowd. Tobacco organizations influence these stages to make drawing in satisfied, run intuitive missions, and fabricate networks around their brands. The visual idea of stages like Instagram has been taken advantage of to feature smoking as a direction for living, adding to the standardization of tobacco use.

Managing on the web and virtual entertainment advancement presents remarkable difficulties because of the worldwide and dynamic nature of these stages. Stricter guidelines are important to address the business' capacity to adjust and take advantage of arising on the web spaces for limited time purposes.

Guideline and Countermeasures:

Perceiving the mischief brought about by the techniques utilized by the tobacco business in promoting and publicizing, administrative measures have been executed universally to check the business' impact. The World Wellbeing Association's Structure Show on Tobacco Control (FCTC) addresses an extensive global work to address tobacco-related issues, including promoting and publicizing.

Realistic admonition names on cigarette bundles, limitations on tobacco publicizing in conventional media, and prohibitions on tobacco sponsorship of sports and far-reaching developments are instances of administrative measures that mean to restrict the effect of industry advancement. In any case, the viability of these actions changes, and there is a consistent need to adjust guidelines to new showcasing channels and techniques.

Countermarketing efforts have arisen as an integral asset in the battle against tobacco industry advancement. These missions mean to challenge the business' messages, expose fantasies around smoking, and make elective accounts. They frequently use strong visuals, individual tributes, and online entertainment to arrive at interest groups, especially youth.

Instructive drives in schools and networks assume a vital part in bringing issues to light about the strategies utilized by the tobacco business. By enabling people with information about the manipulative idea of tobacco advertising, these drives add to building versatility against the business' impact.

The examination concerning the techniques utilized by the tobacco business in promoting and publicizing uncovers a perplexing and multi-layered scene. Designated showcasing, sponsorship and advancement, retail location strategies, and online systems are painstakingly arranged to keep up with and extend the business' piece of the pie. The steadiness and flexibility of these strategies highlight the continuous test of shielding general wellbeing from the damages of tobacco use.

Administrative measures and countermarketing endeavors address fundamental devices in this continuous fight. Stricter guidelines that cover arising publicizing channels, combined with inventive countermarketing efforts, are important to check the business' impact. Instructive drives that engage people to basically assess showcasing messages and go with informed decisions add to building a general public less powerless to the manipulative strategies of the tobacco business.

As the tobacco scene keeps on developing, with new items and promoting channels arising, the requirement for dynamic and responsive tobacco control measures turns out to be progressively obvious. The aggregate endeavors of policymakers, general wellbeing supporters, instructors, and networks are fundamental to establishing a climate that shields people, especially the adolescent, from the tricky procedures of the tobacco business. By getting it, trying, and controlling the strategies utilized in promoting and publicizing, society can pursue a future liberated from the unavoidable damages of tobacco use.

4.2 Explore the controversial history of tobacco companies and their impact on public health.

Investigating the dubious history of tobacco organizations and their effect on general wellbeing uncovers an intricate story set apart by many years of control, disavowal, and protection from guidelines pointed toward checking the staggering wellbeing impacts of tobacco use. From the early promoting efforts that glamorized smoking to the cutting edge difficulties presented by new tobacco items, the business' activities have had significant results on worldwide general wellbeing.

Early Showcasing and Glamorization:
The starting points of the questionable history of tobacco organizations can be followed back to the mid twentieth century while smoking was socially OK as well as frequently depicted as charming and modern. Tobacco organizations participated in forceful advertising efforts that

connected smoking to ideas of polish, opportunity, and advancement. Famous figures, including entertainers and competitors, were enrolled to underwrite cigarette brands, making a strong relationship among smoking and achievement.

Cigarette commercials frequently included deluding wellbeing claims, introducing smoking as an innocuous or even wellbeing advancing action. The well known "Lights of Opportunity" crusade during the 1920s, organized by Edward Bernays, expected to break the cultural no against ladies smoking openly. Bernays, a trailblazer in advertising, decisively connected smoking with thoughts of female strengthening, further settling in smoking in the social texture.

Control of Logical Proof:

As proof connecting smoking to wellbeing chances started to arise, the tobacco business answered with a mission of disavowal and control. Rather than recognizing the mounting logical agreement, tobacco organizations effectively attempted to make uncertainty around the wellbeing impacts of smoking. They financed research projects that intended to raise serious questions about the laid out interface among smoking and infections like cellular breakdown in the lungs and coronary illness.

The business' control of logical proof stretched out to the purposeful concealment of inside research discoveries. Archives delivered through suit and informants have uncovered examples where tobacco organizations knew about the unsafe impacts of their items however decided to hide this data. The notorious "Tobacco Papers" uncovered a purposeful work to minimize the dangers and keep up with public disarray.

Forceful Resistance to Guideline:

As consciousness of the wellbeing chances related with smoking developed, administrative measures were proposed to control tobacco utilization. In any case, the tobacco business answered with fervent resistance to any type of guideline. Campaigning endeavors, political commitments, and lawful difficulties became signs of the business' procedure to oppose government mediation.

Outstandingly, the business battled against noticeable strategies, for example, advance notice marks on cigarette bundles, limitations on promoting, and impediments on smoking in broad daylight places. Tobacco organizations contended against these actions, frequently utilizing the way of talking of individual decision and individual flexibility. The resistance to guideline mirrored the business' assurance to safeguard its benefits to the detriment of general wellbeing.

Focusing on Weak Populaces:

One of the most hostile parts of the tobacco business' set of experiences is its designated promoting towards weak populaces. Whether through racially custom fitted publicizing or the essential arrangement of tobacco items in low-pay areas, the business has been censured for fueling wellbeing abberations. Minority people group, including African Americans and Hispanic populaces, have been excessively impacted by tobacco-related sicknesses because of designated showcasing endeavors.

Furthermore, the business has a past filled with forcefully showcasing to youth, regardless of lawful limitations on promoting to minors. Seasoned cigarettes, vivid bundling, and sponsorships of youth-situated occasions have all been utilized to draw in new, frequently underage, smokers. This deliberate focusing of weak populaces has had sweeping results on general wellbeing, adding to wellbeing disparities and fueling the weight of tobacco-related sicknesses in underestimated networks.

Worldwide Development and Impact:

The dubious history of tobacco organizations stretches out past public boundaries, with the business effectively looking for new business sectors and impacting worldwide strategy. As smoking rates declined in big time salary nations because of expanded attention to wellbeing gambles, the tobacco business moved its concentration to developing business sectors in low-and center pay nations. Forceful showcasing efforts, careless guidelines, and exchange rehearses have added to increasing smoking rates in these areas.

The business' impact on worldwide strategy has been especially apparent in endeavors to sabotage global tobacco control measures. Economic deals and lawful difficulties have been utilized to challenge guidelines, making an intricate snare of monetary interests that occasionally supplant general wellbeing contemplations.

The worldwide development of tobacco organizations has brought up moral issues about corporate obligation and the requirement for deliberate global endeavors to address the effect on general wellbeing.

Item Advancement and Mischief Decrease:

Because of expanding investigation and declining smoking rates, the tobacco business has sought after item development for of supporting its portion of the overall industry. Smokeless tobacco, e-cigarettes, and warmed tobacco items have been presented as choices, with the business advancing these items as possibly less hurtful than customary cigarettes. This has prompted banters about the job of damage decrease systems in general wellbeing.

Pundits contend that the business' emphasis on hurt decrease is an essential move to keep up with dependence and benefits. While some mischief decrease advocates support the utilization of elective items for the purpose of progressing away from smoking, concerns stay about the drawn out wellbeing impacts and industry inspirations. Finding some kind of harmony between hurt decrease and forestalling tobacco industry double-dealing is a mind boggling challenge confronting general wellbeing endeavors.

Suit and Responsibility:

The dubious history of tobacco organizations has been accentuated via milestone fights in court and suit. People hurt by tobacco-related infections, as well as state run administrations looking for remuneration for medical care costs, have prosecuted tobacco organizations. The Expert Settlement Understanding in the US, came to in the last part of the 1990s, denoted a critical defining moment, with significant tobacco organizations consenting to pay billions of dollars to settle claims and asset hostile to smoking efforts.

In spite of lawful triumphs and expanded consciousness of the business' underhanded works on, considering tobacco organizations responsible remaining parts a complicated and continuous test. The business' abundant resources, lawful moving, and worldwide impact make obstacles for people and states looking for equity and remuneration.

General Wellbeing Efforts and Progress:

While the dubious history of tobacco organizations is set apart by trickiness and protection from guideline, there have been striking accomplishments in general wellbeing efforts. Hostile to smoking drives, realistic admonition names, and expanded familiarity with the risks of tobacco use have added to a decrease in smoking rates in numerous nations. Sans smoke strategies, expanded charges on tobacco items, and thorough general wellbeing efforts play played essential parts in moving cultural mentalities towards smoking.

The execution of the Structure Show on Tobacco Control (FCTC) by the World Wellbeing Association addresses a worldwide work to address tobacco-related issues all in all. Sanctioned by various nations, the FCTC gives a structure to exhaustive tobacco control measures, stressing the requirement for global participation to battle the business' effect on general wellbeing.

The questionable history of tobacco organizations and their effect on general wellbeing is a mind boggling embroidery of showcasing procedures, logical control, and protection from guideline. From the early glamorization of smoking to the worldwide extension and focusing of weak populaces, the business' activities have had broad results on general wellbeing.

Endeavors to address the effect of tobacco organizations require a diverse methodology. Stricter guidelines, thorough general wellbeing efforts, worldwide participation, and legitimate responsibility are fundamental parts of the battle against the tobacco business' impact. Understanding the authentic setting and gaining from past difficulties are urgent for molding compelling strategies and intercessions that focus on general wellbeing over corporate interests.

While progress has been made in diminishing smoking rates and expanding mindfulness, the fight against the tobacco business' effect on general wellbeing is continuous. Proceeded with cautiousness, development in tobacco control measures, and a promise to prove based strategies are fundamental for making a future where the staggering wellbeing impacts of tobacco use are limited, and general wellbeing is focused on over corporate benefit.

Chapter 5

The Battle for Regulation

The fight for guideline with regards to tobacco control addresses an extended and complex battle between general wellbeing advocates and the strong tobacco industry. This continuous struggle has been described by endeavors to execute and fortify guidelines pointed toward checking the antagonistic wellbeing impacts of tobacco use, countered by the business' opposition through campaigning, lawful difficulties, and endeavors to shape general assessment. Inspecting the set of experiences and elements of this fight gives bits of knowledge into the difficulties confronted, the advancement accomplished, and the continuous requirement for strong administrative structures.

Authentic Outline:

The underlying foundations of the fight for guideline can be followed back to the mid-twentieth century when logical proof connecting smoking to serious wellbeing chances started to amass. The Top health spokesperson's Report in the US in 1964 denoted a turning point, unequivocally expressing the connection among smoking and cellular breakdown in the lungs. This original report established the groundwork for administrative endeavors worldwide, setting off a change in outlook in open discernment and making ready for hostile to smoking drives.

Early Administrative Endeavors:

In the repercussions of the Top health spokesperson's Report, nations began to acquaint measures with direct tobacco promoting, limit smoking out in the open places, and command cautioning names on cigarette bundles. Notwithstanding, these early administrative endeavors confronted critical resistance from the tobacco business. Campaigning efforts, lawful difficulties, and advertising endeavors were sent to oppose guidelines that undermined the business' benefit.

One outstanding improvement during this period was the formation of the World Wellbeing Association's System Show on Tobacco Control (FCTC), took on in 2003. The FCTC addressed a milestone worldwide settlement, giving a thorough structure to worldwide tobacco control endeavors. In spite of its importance, the FCTC confronted difficulties in execution, with the tobacco business proceeding with its obstruction on numerous fronts.

Tobacco Industry Strategies:

The fight for guideline has been portrayed by a scope of strategies utilized by the tobacco business to subvert and debilitate proposed measures. These strategies incorporate forceful campaigning, subsidizing political missions, testing guidelines in court, and participating in advertising endeavors to shape popular assessment.

Campaigning and Political Impact:

One of the essential strategies utilized by the tobacco business is broad campaigning to impact administrators and policymakers. This includes monetary commitments to political missions, direct commitment with administrators, and the foundation of associations with persuasive policymakers. By utilizing its monetary power, the business looks to shape guidelines in support of its and forestall the entry of measures that could affect its benefits.

Legitimate Difficulties:

The tobacco business has reliably turned to legitimate difficulties for of blocking administrative measures. Claims have been recorded against advance notice marks, promoting limitations, and plain bundling prerequisites, among different guidelines. The business frequently contends that such measures encroach on its on the whole correct to free discourse or obstruct its capacity to direct business. These fights in court make deterrents for administrative organizations and can prompt delayed defers in the execution of essential general wellbeing measures.

Advertising Endeavors:

To impact general assessment and fabricate resistance to proposed guidelines, the tobacco business has put vigorously in advertising efforts. These missions frequently utilize strategies to make light of the wellbeing dangers of smoking, depict the business as a safeguard of individual opportunities, and raise issue about the logical agreement on tobacco-related hurt. By molding public insight, the business means to earn support against administrative drives.

Triumphs and Misfortunes:

The fight for guideline has seen the two triumphs and misfortunes throughout the long term. Victories incorporate the execution of sans smoke strategies, expansions in tobacco charges, and the presentation of realistic advance notice names on cigarette bundles in different nations. These actions have added to diminished smoking rates and expanded public consciousness of the damages related with tobacco use.

In any case, mishaps have happened, especially when administrative endeavors serious areas of strength for face from the tobacco business. Legitimate difficulties have prompted postponements and rollbacks of particular measures, and the business' capacity to adjust to arising items, like e-cigarettes, has introduced new difficulties for controllers. Finding some kind of harmony between tending to the dangers of conventional tobacco items and managing novel items stays a dynamic and developing part of tobacco control.

Worldwide Participation:

The fight for guideline isn't restricted to individual nations; a worldwide test requires global participation. The FCTC addresses a cooperative exertion by the global local area to address tobacco-related issues all in all. Sanctioned by various nations, the FCTC frames rules for tobacco control approaches, including publicizing and advancement boycotts, bundling and naming prerequisites, and measures to safeguard non-smokers from openness to tobacco smoke.

Notwithstanding the FCTC's importance, challenges continue accomplishing uniform execution across all nations. The tobacco business' worldwide reach, combined with varieties in financial and political settings, makes it hard to lay out reliable and vigorous administrative structures around the world.

Arising Items and Administrative Difficulties:

The coming of new tobacco and nicotine items, like e-cigarettes and warmed tobacco items, has introduced novel difficulties for controllers. While these items are frequently advertised as options in contrast to customary cigarettes and, surprisingly, as smoking suspension helps, worries about their wellbeing and potential to draw in new, particularly youthful, clients have provoked calls for administrative examination.

Controlling arising items requires a nuanced approach that considers hurt decrease potential while forestalling unseen side-effects, for example, item use inception among non-smokers. Finding some kind of harmony includes progressing research, observing industry rehearses, and adjusting guidelines to stay up with innovative headways.

General Wellbeing Backing and Training:

In the fight for guideline, general wellbeing backing and training assume significant parts in gathering support for administrative measures and countering industry stories. Promotion endeavors include assembling networks, drawing in with policymakers, and raising public mindfulness about the damages of tobacco use. These drives try to engage people to help and request viable guidelines that focus on general wellbeing.

Schooling is a foundation of tobacco control endeavors, intending to illuminate people in general about the dangers related with tobacco use, the strategies utilized by the business, and the advantages of administrative measures. By encouraging a very much educated and drew out in the open, tobacco control backers can gather speed for strategies that shield people and networks from the damages of tobacco.

Monetary Contemplations and Industry Impact:

The fight for guideline is frequently snared with financial contemplations, remembering worries about employment misfortunes for the tobacco business and the likely effect on nearby economies. The tobacco business decisively stresses these financial variables to influence general assessment and impact policymakers. Offsetting general wellbeing goals with financial contemplations is an intricate test that requires smart strategy draws near and the investigation of option monetary open doors for impacted networks.

The Job of Innovation and Computerized Advertising:

In the computerized age, innovation and online stages have become huge fields in the fight for guideline. The tobacco business uses computerized promoting systems to contact expansive crowds, particularly youth, through web-based entertainment, powerhouse coordinated efforts, and intelligent missions. Directing internet promoting presents exceptional difficulties, requiring inventive ways to deal with address the unique idea of computerized stages and keep the business from taking advantage of new roads.

The Significance of Complete Approaches:

The fight for guideline highlights the significance of complete and prove based arrangements that address different parts of tobacco use. Viable guidelines incorporate promoting and showcasing limitations, without smoke arrangements, tax assessment procedures, and measures to forestall youth inception. An exhaustive methodology perceives the interconnected idea of these parts and tries to make a synergistic effect on lessening tobacco-related hurt.

The fight for guideline in tobacco control is a dynamic and progressing battle that unfurls on numerous fronts. From early endeavors to battle smoking to contemporary difficulties presented by arising items and globalized advertising, the administrative scene keeps on advancing. Triumphs in diminishing smoking rates and executing compelling arrangements are tempered by the tireless opposition of the tobacco business, requiring proceeded with watchfulness and variation by general wellbeing backers and policymakers.

Accomplishing significant advancement in tobacco control requires a diverse methodology that incorporates powerful guidelines, worldwide participation, general wellbeing support, and continuous schooling. Offsetting financial contemplations with general wellbeing goals, tending to the impact of innovation and advanced advertising, and expecting difficulties presented by arising items are basic parts of exploring the mind boggling landscape of tobacco guideline.

As the fight for guideline unfurls, a definitive objective remaining parts the security of general wellbeing and the decrease of the staggering effect of tobacco use on people and networks. By gaining from past difficulties, remaining receptive to industry strategies, and embracing proof based approaches, society can pursue a future where viable guidelines win, and the damages of tobacco are limited for the prosperity of present and people in the future.

5.1 Chart the efforts to regulate tobacco, from early warnings to present-day policies.

Outlining the endeavors to control tobacco, from early admonitions to introduce day strategies, gives a verifiable point of view on the perplexing and progressing fight to safeguard general wellbeing from the damages of tobacco use. This excursion envelops achievements like early logical disclosures, the foundation of administrative structures, and the advancing difficulties presented by the tobacco business' opposition, arising items, and worldwide elements.

Early Admonitions and Logical Disclosures:

The course of events of endeavors to manage tobacco starts with early logical alerts about the wellbeing chances related with smoking. The milestone Top health spokesperson's Report in the US in 1964 denoted a defining moment, openly recognizing the connection among smoking and serious medical issue like cellular breakdown in the lungs and coronary illness. This report established the groundwork for resulting administrative activities and hostile to smoking drives around the world.

As logical proof mounted, nations all over the planet started endeavors to advise the general population about the dangers regarding tobacco use. Public mindfulness crusades, frequently highlighting realistic wellbeing admonitions, planned to teach people about the risks of smoking and make a social change in discernments encompassing tobacco. These early alerts set up for additional complete administrative measures to come.

Promoting Limitations and Cautioning Marks:

One of the underlying administrative reactions to the wellbeing dangers of tobacco was the burden of limitations on promoting and the presentation of caution names on cigarette bundles. Nations started to restrict the manners by which tobacco items could be promoted, perceiving the job of publicizing in tempting new smokers, especially the young.

Cautioning names, highlighting realistic pictures and wellbeing messages, turned into a significant device in passing the wellbeing gambles straightforwardly on to customers. These names expected to check the business' promoting endeavors by furnishing people with clear data about the likely results of tobacco use. The execution of publicizing limitations and cautioning marks addressed a critical stage in engaging people to go with informed decisions about smoking.

Sans smoke Approaches:

Perceiving the risks of handed-down cigarette smoke and the significance of safeguarding non-smokers, endeavors were attempted to carry out without smoke approaches in broad daylight spaces and work environments. The objective was to establish conditions where people could reside, work, and associate without openness to the hurtful impacts of tobacco smoke.

The execution of without smoke strategies denoted a change in perspective in general wellbeing ways to deal with tobacco control. It not just intended to safeguard non-smokers from the risks of detached smoking yet in addition added to switching normal practices up smoking. Sans smoke approaches collected far reaching support and exhibited the practicality of administrative measures in encouraging better open spaces.

Tax assessment Techniques:

Tax collection has arisen as a strong administrative instrument to control tobacco use. By expanding the cost of tobacco items through charges, states try to decrease utilization, particularly among cost delicate populaces like youth and low-pay people. More exorbitant costs make tobacco items more expensive and act as an obstacle to both commencement and smoked.

Tax collection systems have demonstrated compelling in diminishing smoking rates and producing income for general wellbeing drives. In any case, they have additionally confronted resistance from the tobacco business, which frequently contends against charge increments by featuring expected financial effects and sneaking worries. In spite of these difficulties, tax collection stays a foundation of far reaching tobacco control strategies.

System Show on Tobacco Control (FCTC):

The global local area perceived the requirement for a planned worldwide reaction to the difficulties presented by tobacco, prompting the making of the World Wellbeing Association's System Show on Tobacco Control (FCTC). Taken on in 2003, the FCTC addresses an achievement in worldwide endeavors to control tobacco.

The FCTC frames a bunch of rules and measures to address different parts of tobacco control, including publicizing and advancement boycotts, bundling and naming necessities, and insurance from openness to tobacco smoke. Confirmed by various nations, the FCTC fills in as a plan for worldwide collaboration in fighting the tobacco plague. Nonetheless, challenges continue accomplishing general execution and defeating industry opposition.

Arising Items and Administrative Difficulties:

The scene of tobacco guideline has become progressively mind boggling with the rise of new items, like e-cigarettes and warmed tobacco items. These items, frequently advertised as options in contrast to conventional cigarettes, have presented administrative difficulties because of inquiries regarding their wellbeing, appeal to youth, and expected influence on smoking suspension endeavors.

Managing arising items requires a dynamic and versatile methodology that considers hurt decrease potential while forestalling unseen side-effects. Finding some kind of harmony includes progressing research, checking industry practices, and refreshing guidelines to address the developing scene of tobacco utilization.

Realistic Admonition Names and Plain Bundling:

Expanding on the progress of early advance notice names, a few nations have gone to administrative lengths further by carrying out realistic advance notice marks on cigarette bundles. These marks utilize strong visuals to pass the wellbeing dangers of smoking and point on to make a more grounded influence on customer conduct. Moreover, the idea of plain bundling, which eliminates marking components and normalizes the presence of cigarette bundles, has built up momentum for of diminishing the allure of tobacco items.

Realistic admonition names and plain bundling address inventive ways to deal with improving the viability of wellbeing alerts and limiting the impact of advertising on buyer decisions. These actions recognize the requirement for consistent development in administrative systems to address the complex strategies utilized by the tobacco business.

Worldwide Financial and Exchange Elements:

The endeavors to control tobacco are not confined from more extensive monetary and exchange elements. The tobacco business' worldwide reach has prompted worries about the expected impact of economic accords on tobacco control measures. Exchange questions and lawful difficulties have emerged as tobacco organizations try to safeguard their inclinations by testing guidelines that they see as obstacles to streamlined commerce.

Exploring the crossing point of worldwide financial elements and tobacco guideline requires a cautious difficult exercise. Policymakers should think about the effect of guidelines on nearby economies, while additionally focusing on general wellbeing goals. Finding some kind of harmony includes investigating elective financial open doors for impacted networks and pushing for strategies that focus on wellbeing over industry interests.

Advanced Advertising and Online Difficulties:

The approach of the advanced age has presented new difficulties in managing tobacco, especially with the ascent of web based showcasing and online business. The tobacco business has adjusted to advanced stages, utilizing online entertainment, powerhouse coordinated efforts, and intelligent missions to contact wide crowds, including youth. Controlling internet showcasing presents one of a kind difficulties because of the worldwide and dynamic nature of computerized stages.

Endeavors to address online moves include refreshing guidelines to cover arising advertising channels, checking industry practices, and utilizing computerized stages for hostile to smoking efforts. Controllers should stay cautious to keep the business from taking advantage of new roads and bypassing conventional promoting limitations.

General Wellbeing Promotion and Training:

The progress of tobacco guideline endeavors is entwined with vigorous general wellbeing backing and schooling drives. Backing efforts activate networks, draw in with policymakers, and raise public mindfulness about the damages of tobacco use. These endeavors mean to make a groundswell of help for administrative measures and counter industry stories.

Instruction stays a foundation of tobacco control, enabling people with data about the dangers of smoking, the strategies utilized by the business, and the advantages of administrative measures. Schools, people group, and medical care suppliers assume essential parts in dispersing information and encouraging a very much educated public that effectively supports and requests compelling tobacco control strategies.

Difficulties and Future Headings:

In spite of huge advancement in tobacco guideline, challenges continue. The tobacco business' tenacious obstruction, the rise of new items, and the worldwide idea of the tobacco exchange make progressing obstacles for general wellbeing supporters and policymakers. Accomplishing a without tobacco future requires a multi-layered approach that locations developing industry strategies, adjusts to innovative headways, and remains sensitive to arising difficulties.

Future headings in tobacco guideline might include reinforcing worldwide participation, especially in authorizing the arrangements of the FCTC. Development in administrative systems, for example, bridling innovation for more successful implementation, and tending to the financial contemplations related with tobacco control are significant parts of diagramming a course forward.

5.2 Explore the challenges faced by governments and public health organizations in curbing tobacco use.

Investigating the difficulties looked by states and general wellbeing associations in controling tobacco use uncovers a multi-layered scene set apart by industry strategies, financial contemplations, developing items, and the requirement for exhaustive administrative systems. In spite of critical advancement in tobacco control, diligent impediments keep on testing the purpose of policymakers and general wellbeing advocates in their quest for a sans tobacco future.

Industry Strategies and Resistance:

A huge test in controling tobacco use is the impressive resistance presented by the tobacco business. With significant monetary assets, political impact, and modern promoting methodologies, tobacco organizations effectively oppose administrative measures that compromise their benefits. Campaigning, legitimate difficulties, and advertising efforts are conveyed to sabotage and defer strategies pointed toward decreasing tobacco utilization.

Campaigning and Political Impact:

Tobacco organizations utilize broad campaigning endeavors to impact administrators and policymakers, meaning to shape regulation in support of themselves. Monetary commitments to political missions, commitment with powerful figures, and utilizing industry-accommodating accounts are normal strategies. The business' political impact makes obstacles for the execution of vigorous tobacco control strategies, as policymakers might confront clashing tensions between general wellbeing objectives and industry interests.

Lawful Difficulties:

Lawful difficulties address a persevering obstruction in the administrative scene of tobacco control. The business frequently documents claims against proposed guidelines, refering to issues like free discourse infringement or financial effects. Fights in court can bring about delayed delays, alterations to arrangements, or, now and again, the striking down of guidelines through and through. The asset escalated nature of judicial actions puts an extra weight on legislatures and general wellbeing associations trying to implement compelling tobacco control measures.

Advertising Efforts:

The tobacco business puts vigorously in advertising efforts to shape popular assessment and construct resistance to administrative drives. These missions frequently minimize the wellbeing dangers of smoking, underscore individual decision, and question the logical agreement on tobacco-related hurt. By affecting public discernment, the business expects to accumulate support against arrangements that could influence its main concern.

Monetary Contemplations and Employment Cutback Concerns:

Offsetting general wellbeing targets with financial contemplations represents a huge test for legislatures looking to check tobacco use. The tobacco business is much of the time profoundly imbued in neighborhood economies, giving position and adding to burden incomes. Policymakers face the sensitive errand of tending to tobacco-related wellbeing worries while alleviating possible monetary repercussions, for example, employment misfortunes in tobacco-creating areas.

Elective Monetary Open doors:

Effectively tending to the monetary difficulties of tobacco control requires the distinguishing proof and advancement of option financial open doors for networks generally dependent on tobacco creation. Broadening of neighborhood economies, interests in manageable horticulture, and backing for businesses irrelevant to tobacco are critical parts of a far reaching technique that limits the financial effect on impacted networks.

Tobacco Industry's Monetary Impact:

The monetary impact of the tobacco business reaches out past individual networks to more extensive public and global settings. The business decisively underscores the monetary commitments it makes, contending against tough guidelines on the grounds of potential employment misfortunes and antagonistic financial impacts. State run administrations face the test of opposing industry strain while focusing on general wellbeing objectives.

Globalization and Exchange Elements:

In a time of globalization, the tobacco business' scope reaches out across borders, impacting exchange elements and worldwide relations. Economic alliance and settlements can at times be utilized by the business to challenge guidelines considered adverse to its inclinations. The crossing point of worldwide exchange and tobacco control requires cautious route to forestall exchange related difficulties from obstructing the execution of powerful administrative measures.

Exchange Questions and Lawful Difficulties:

Tobacco organizations have been known to start exchange questions and lawful difficulties against nations carrying out severe tobacco control measures. These difficulties might be outlined as infringement of economic accords or licensed innovation freedoms. The possible monetary and lawful outcomes of such debates establish a mind boggling climate for legislatures meaning to focus on general wellbeing over industry interests.

Global Collaboration:

Tending to the difficulties presented by globalization and exchange elements requires worldwide participation. Cooperative endeavors, for example, the execution of the System Show on Tobacco Control (FCTC), give a structure to nations to cooperate in managing tobacco. Notwithstanding, challenges stay in accomplishing reliable execution across all countries and keeping the tobacco business from taking advantage of global economic accords.

Arising Items and Novel Difficulties:

The scene of tobacco use has developed with the presentation of new items, like e-cigarettes and warmed tobacco gadgets. These items, frequently advertised as options in contrast to conventional cigarettes, present novel difficulties for controllers. The tobacco business' capacity to adjust and improve requires a powerful way to deal with address the special dangers related with arising items.

Youth Allure and Engaging quality:

E-cigarettes and seasoned tobacco items, with their different scope of flavors and smooth plans, have acquired notoriety among youth. The business' capacity to showcase these items as stylish and less destructive postures difficulties in forestalling youth commencement. Controllers should consider the extraordinary allure of these items to various socio-economics and execute measures to check their openness and engaging quality to youth.

Wellbeing Cases and Mischief Decrease:

The development of items promoted as mischief decrease instruments, for example, e-cigarettes, brings up issues about their wellbeing and via-bility. Controllers face the test of finding some kind of harmony between recognizing the potential damage decrease benefits for laid out smokers while keeping these items from becoming door items for non-smokers, especially youth.

Administrative Flexibility:

The fast speed of development in the tobacco business requests admin-istrative versatility. Controllers should keep up to date with arising items, evaluate their wellbeing dangers, and update guidelines appropriately. Ac-complishing this equilibrium requires progressing research, cooperation with general wellbeing specialists, and the capacity to answer quickly to changes in the tobacco market.

Instructive Difficulties and Mindfulness Holes:

Regardless of far and wide attention to the wellbeing gambles related with tobacco use, there are constant provokes in successfully impart-ing this data to different populaces. Instructive drives face obstacles in arriving at explicit socioeconomics, countering industry stories, and tending to social factors that impact tobacco use.

Social Discernments and Normal practices:

Tobacco use is many times implanted in social practices, and normal practices can assume a huge part in deeply shaping individual way of behaving. Instructive endeavors should explore social discernments encompassing tobacco, tending to the foundations of smoking inside unambiguous networks, and cultivating a change in normal practices towards sans tobacco ways of life.

Designated Promoting and Weak Populaces:

The designated advertising of tobacco items, particularly towards weak populaces, presents difficulties for instructive drives. Minority people group, low-pay people, and youth are frequently excessively impacted by tobacco-related wellbeing inconsistencies. Instructive missions should be custom fitted to address the particular difficulties looked by these populaces and check industry strategies that exploit weaknesses.

Computerized Education and Online Difficulties:

In the computerized age, online stages and virtual entertainment have become compelling channels for data scattering. Controllers face moves in elevating advanced education to assist individuals with fundamentally assessing on the web content connected with tobacco use. Moreover, tending to the business' utilization of advanced stages for advertising and affecting youth requires creative procedures to explore the internet based scene.

Checking and Requirement:

Successful guideline of tobacco requires strong checking and authorization instruments. Legislatures and general wellbeing associations should fight with difficulties connected with asset limitations, industry disruption, and the requirement for constant transformation to arising patterns.

Asset Limitations:

Restricted assets, both human and monetary, can frustrate the capacity of administrative bodies to screen and implement tobacco control gauges really. Satisfactory subsidizing, staffing, and mechanical foundation are fundamental for supported endeavors in checking consistence and answering industry strategies.

Industry Disruption and Illegal Exchange:

The tobacco business' endeavors to undermine guidelines, combined with the potential for illegal exchange tobacco items, present difficulties for checking and requirement. Controllers should be watchful against strategies like pirating, falsifying, and misleading showcasing rehearses that avoid existing guidelines.

Worldwide Coordination and Data Sharing:

Given the worldwide idea of the tobacco business and the interconnectedness of business sectors, coordination and data dividing among nations are fundamental. Cooperative endeavors to share best practices, knowledge on industry strategies, and fruitful implementation methodologies can upgrade the adequacy of administrative measures.

Complete Administrative Structures:

The intricacy of difficulties in controling tobacco use highlights the significance of extensive administrative structures. Compelling guideline requires a coordinated methodology that tends to different parts of tobacco control, from publicizing limitations to tax assessment arrangements and instructive drives.

Comprehensive Methodologies:

Policymakers and general wellbeing associations should take on all encompassing methodologies that perceive the interconnected idea of tobacco control measures. A blend of administrative instruments, including promoting limitations, sans smoke strategies, tax collection, and instructive missions, can make a synergistic effect on decreasing tobacco use.

Proof Based Independent direction:

Administrative structures should be educated by proof based independent direction. Continuous exploration on the wellbeing impacts of tobacco items, the effect of administrative measures, and arising patterns in tobacco use is essential for molding compelling strategies that answer the developing scene.

Public-Private Associations:

Joint effort between state run administrations, general wellbeing associations, and non-legislative elements is fundamental for successful tobacco control. Public-private organizations that draw in with the confidential area, including businesses irrelevant to tobacco, can add to shared goals in decreasing tobacco use while regarding financial contemplations.

The difficulties looked by legislatures and general wellbeing associations in checking tobacco use are perplexing and multi-layered. From industry resistance and monetary contemplations to arising items and instructive holes, the scene of tobacco control requests inventive and versatile methodologies.

Tending to these difficulties requires supported responsibility, global participation, and an acknowledgment of the requirement for exhaustive administrative systems. Policymakers and general wellbeing advocates should explore the complicated elements of industry impact, financial contemplations, and developing items to make a future where tobacco-related hurt is limited, and general wellbeing overshadows industry interests. Regardless of the obstacles, progress in tobacco control stays reachable through deliberate endeavors that focus on the prosperity of people and networks all over the planet.

Chapter 6

Tobacco and Health

Tobacco use presents critical and extensive wellbeing gambles, affecting people, networks, and worldwide general wellbeing. The association among tobacco and a horde of medical problems has been broadly recorded, prompting far and wide endeavors to bring issues to light, carry out administrative measures, and backing discontinuance drives. This investigation digs into the mind boggling interchange among tobacco and wellbeing, looking at the direct physiological impacts of tobacco use, the connection among tobacco and different sicknesses, and the more extensive general wellbeing suggestions.

Physiological Impacts of Tobacco:

The physiological impacts of tobacco use are significant and include different organ frameworks, with nicotine, the essential psychoactive part of tobacco, assuming a focal part.

Nicotine Fixation and the Mind:

Nicotine, a profoundly drug, follows up on the mind's prize framework, delivering synapses like dopamine. This makes a supporting cycle that adds to the improvement of enslavement. People who use tobacco routinely may find it trying to stop because of the neurological changes related with nicotine reliance.

Cardiovascular Framework Effect:

Tobacco use affects the cardiovascular framework. Nicotine raises pulse and circulatory strain, while different synthetics in tobacco smoke can harm veins and add to the development of atherosclerotic plaques. These progressions increment the gamble of coronary illness, stroke, and other cardiovascular confusions.

Respiratory Framework Results:

The respiratory framework endures the worst part of tobacco's effect, especially in people who smoke. The inward breath of tobacco smoke opens the lungs to a poisonous blend of synthetic substances, prompting irritation, disabled lung capability, and an expanded defenselessness to respiratory diseases. Ongoing obstructive aspiratory sickness (COPD) and cellular breakdown in the lungs are among the extreme respiratory outcomes of long haul smoking.

Malignant growth Hazard:

Tobacco use is a main source of different tumors, with smoking being the essential gamble factor for cellular breakdown in the lungs. Past the lungs, tobacco smoke contains cancer-causing agents that can prompt diseases of the mouth, throat, throat, pancreas, bladder, and then some. Smokeless tobacco items likewise increment the gamble of oral, esophageal, and pancreatic tumors.

Conceptive and Fetal Wellbeing:

Tobacco use unfavorably affects regenerative wellbeing in all kinds of people. In men, smoking can add to erectile brokenness and lessen sperm quality. In ladies, tobacco use is connected to difficulties during pregnancy, including preterm birth, low birth weight, and expanded chance of abrupt baby demise disorder (SIDS). Openness to handed-down cigarette smoke during pregnancy can make comparable hindering impacts.

Connecting Tobacco to Significant Medical problems:

The relationship between tobacco use and significant medical problems stretches out past individual wellbeing results to more extensive general wellbeing challenges.

Cardiovascular Infections:

Cardiovascular infections address a main source of mortality universally, and tobacco use is a significant supporter of this scourge. Smoking builds the gamble of coronary illness, stroke, and fringe vascular sickness. The cardiovascular effect of tobacco use puts a significant weight on medical services frameworks and adds to the worldwide weight of non-transferable sicknesses.

Respiratory Sicknesses:

Tobacco use is an essential driver of respiratory sicknesses, including constant bronchitis and emphysema, by and large known as ongoing obstructive pneumonic infection (COPD). COPD is described by moderate wind stream constraint and is a significant wellspring of bleakness and mortality. The monetary and medical care loads related with COPD are huge, influencing the two people and society in general.

Malignant growth Weight:

The connection between tobacco use and malignant growth is deep rooted, with smoking representing a significant extent of disease cases around the world. Cellular breakdown in the lungs, specifically, is firmly connected with tobacco smoking, and endeavors to decrease tobacco-related tumors frequently center around smoking anticipation and end. Malignant growth therapy costs and the cultural effect of disease related dreariness and mortality put an extensive weight on medical services frameworks.

Irresistible Sicknesses:

Tobacco use can intensify the effect of irresistible illnesses. Smokers might be more vulnerable to respiratory diseases, and the immunosuppressive impacts of tobacco smoke can think twice about body's capacity to ward off contaminations. Furthermore, the collective idea of smoking, whether in encased spaces or through shared tobacco items, can add to the spread of irresistible sicknesses.

Psychological wellness Results:

The connection between tobacco use and psychological wellness is mind boggling. While certain people use tobacco as a way of dealing with especially difficult times for pressure or emotional wellness conditions, the general effect of smoking on mental prosperity is pessimistic. Smoking is related with an expanded gamble of misery, nervousness problems, and other emotional well-being issues. Stopping smoking has been displayed to further develop emotional wellness results, featuring the significance of tending to tobacco use in psychological well-being settings.

General Wellbeing Suggestions and Worldwide Difficulties:

The wellbeing ramifications of tobacco use reach out to more extensive general wellbeing challenges, affecting medical services frameworks, economies, and social prosperity.

Financial Weight:

The financial weight of tobacco use is monstrous, including direct medical care costs, lost efficiency because of disease and unexpected passing, and costs connected with tending to the social results of tobacco use. Medical care frameworks are stressed by the therapy of tobacco-related illnesses, redirecting assets from other squeezing wellbeing needs.

Wellbeing Imbalances:

Tobacco use adds to wellbeing imbalances, excessively influencing weak populaces. Financial variables, admittance to instruction, and geographic area can impact tobacco use designs. Addressing wellbeing incongruities connected with tobacco requires designated intercessions that consider the extraordinary difficulties looked by changed networks.

Handed-down cigarette smoke Openness:

Handed-down cigarette smoke, otherwise called detached smoke or natural tobacco smoke, presents wellbeing dangers to non-smokers. Openness to handed-down cigarette smoke is connected to respiratory contaminations, unexpected baby demise condition (SIDS), cardiovascular sicknesses, and cellular breakdown in the lungs in non-smokers. Arrangements advancing without smoke conditions are pivotal in decreasing handed-down cigarette smoke openness and safeguarding general well-being.

Worldwide Tobacco Plague:

Tobacco use comprises a worldwide pestilence with expansive outcomes. The World Wellbeing Association (WHO) assesses that tobacco use is liable for in excess of 8 million passings every year, with the greater part happening in low-and center pay nations. The globalization of the tobacco business and the advertising of tobacco items to new populaces present continuous difficulties for worldwide general wellbeing endeavors.

Anticipation and Suspension Procedures:

Compelling anticipation and discontinuance methodologies are fundamental parts of tending to the worldwide tobacco scourge. General wellbeing efforts, smoking end projects, and arrangements that deter tobacco use assume essential parts in lessening the pervasiveness of smoking. Instructive drives zeroed in on the damages of tobacco use, joined with open and proof based end support, can add to a decrease in smoking rates.

Administrative Measures:

Administrative measures are critical in controlling tobacco-related wellbeing gambles. These actions incorporate promoting limitations, realistic admonition marks on cigarette bundles, tax assessment methodologies to expand the expense of tobacco items, and sans smoke strategies out in the open spaces. The execution and implementation of hearty administrative systems are basic for relieving the wellbeing effect of tobacco use.

Developments in Tobacco Control:

Despite diligent difficulties, inventive ways to deal with tobacco control are arising to address the developing scene of tobacco use.

Innovation Based Mediations:

Innovation based mediations, for example, versatile applications, online stages, and text informing programs, are demonstrating successful in supporting smoking discontinuance endeavors. These apparatuses offer customized help, social intercessions, and constant following of headway, making them available and interesting to different populaces.

Hurt Decrease Techniques:

Hurt decrease techniques, including the advancement of less unsafe nicotine conveyance items like nicotine substitution treatments (NRTs) and electronic cigarettes, certainly stand out enough to be noticed. While disputable, some contend that these procedures can give an extension to stopping to people who can't stop suddenly. Adjusting hurt decrease with forestalling youth inception stays a key test.

Local area Commitment and Backing:

Local area commitment and backing are basic parts of effective tobacco control drives. Enabling people group to advocate for without smoke conditions, partake in enemy of tobacco missions, and backing strategy changes improves the viability of general wellbeing endeavors. Grassroots developments and local area driven drives add to switching accepted practices up tobacco use.

Tobacco use stays a significant worldwide general wellbeing challenge, with significant ramifications for individual wellbeing, medical services frameworks, and cultural prosperity. The physiological impacts of tobacco, its relationship with significant medical problems, and the more extensive general wellbeing suggestions highlight the criticalness of far reaching tobacco control endeavors.

Tending to the complicated interchange among tobacco and wellbeing requires a multi-layered approach incorporating counteraction, end, administrative measures, and imaginative techniques. As the worldwide local area keeps on standing up to the tobacco pandemic, continuous examination, cooperative endeavors, and a guarantee to confirm based mediations are vital in accomplishing a future where the wellbeing effects of tobacco use are limited, and social orders can flourish liberated from the weight of tobacco-related sicknesses.

6.1 Examine the direct health consequences of smoking, including respiratory diseases and cancer.

Inspecting the immediate wellbeing outcomes of smoking uncovers a sobering reality, as tobacco use stays a main source of preventable sicknesses and unexpected passing around the world. Smoking affects different organ frameworks, with respiratory infections and malignant growth being unmistakable among the bunch wellbeing outcomes. This investigation dives into the many-sided connection among smoking and respiratory wellbeing, as well as the deeply grounded interface among smoking and different types of malignant growth.

Respiratory Illnesses:

Smoking applies a negative effect on the respiratory framework, with a scope of sicknesses that can prompt constant horribleness and mortality.

Persistent Obstructive Aspiratory Illness (COPD):

Persistent obstructive pneumonic sickness (COPD) is an aggregate term for ongoing bronchitis and emphysema, the two of which are unequivocally connected with smoking. Constant bronchitis includes aggravation and restricting of the aviation routes, prompting hack, inordinate bodily fluid creation, and trouble relaxing. Emphysema is portrayed by the annihilation of lung tissue, lessening the versatility of the air sacs and blocking wind current. COPD is moderate and irreversible, essentially influencing the personal satisfaction and adding to expanded mortality.

Lung Capability Decline:

Smoking speeds up the normal decrease in lung capability that happens with maturing. The harmful parts of tobacco smoke, including tar and cancer-causing agents, harm the lung tissue and aviation routes, prompting diminished lung capability over the long haul. This decline appears as a decrease in the capacity to breathe in and breathe out air, eventually adding to respiratory side effects and debilitated practice resistance.

Expanded Helplessness to Diseases:

Smokers are more helpless to respiratory diseases, including pneumonia and bronchitis. The compromised resistant reaction in smokers, combined with the harm to the respiratory epithelium brought about by tobacco smoke, establishes a climate helpful for the improvement of contaminations. Respiratory diseases can worsen prior respiratory circumstances and add to a pattern of declining lung wellbeing.

Asthma Intensification:

Smoking has been connected to the intensification of asthma side effects. People with asthma who smoke might encounter more continuous and extreme assaults, as tobacco smoke can set off irritation and bronchoconstriction. Smoking end is vital in overseeing asthma and forestalling further crumbling of lung capability.

Malignant growth:

The connection among smoking and malignant growth is unequivocal, with tobacco use being a significant supporter of a few kinds of disease.

Cellular breakdown in the lungs:

Cellular breakdown in the lungs is the most notable and deadliest outcome of smoking. Most of cellular breakdown in the lungs cases are straightforwardly owing to tobacco smoke, with a solid portion reaction relationship — the more cigarettes smoked and the more drawn out the length of smoking, the higher the gamble. Cellular breakdown in the lungs frequently presents at cutting edge stages, bringing about an unfortunate guess. The cancer-causing agents in tobacco smoke, like benzene and formaldehyde, start hereditary changes in lung cells, prompting the uncontrolled development of malignant cells.

Other Respiratory Tumors:

Notwithstanding cellular breakdown in the lungs, smoking is ensnared in other respiratory malignant growths, including tumors of the larynx, pharynx, and windpipe. These tumors are likewise described by the improvement of threatening cells in the respiratory parcel, driven by the cancer-causing parts of tobacco smoke. The occurrence of these malignant growths is altogether higher in smokers contrasted with non-smokers.

Gastrointestinal Tumors:

Smoking is a perceived gamble factor for tumors past the respiratory framework, including diseases of the throat, stomach, pancreas, and colon. The cancer-causing agents in tobacco smoke can enter the stomach related framework, adding to the advancement of growths in different gastrointestinal organs. Smoking discontinuance assumes a vital part in diminishing the gamble of these diseases.

Bladder Malignant growth:

Smoking is a deep rooted risk factor for bladder malignant growth. The harmful synthetic compounds in tobacco smoke are discharged through the pee, uncovering the coating of the bladder to cancer-causing agents. This ongoing openness can prompt the improvement of dangerous cells in the bladder lining. Stopping smoking has been displayed to lessen the gamble of bladder malignant growth over the long run.

Head and Neck Tumors:

The relationship among smoking and tumors of the head and neck, including the mouth, throat, and larynx, is solid. Tobacco smoke contains various cancer-causing agents that can come into direct contact with the tissues in the oral and pharyngeal areas. Smoking end is pivotal in forestalling and diminishing the gamble of these diseases.

Esophageal Malignant growth:

Smoking is a huge gamble factor for esophageal disease, especially squamous cell carcinoma. The cancer-causing agents in tobacco smoke can straightforwardly harm the cells covering the throat, prompting the advancement of dangerous cells. Smoking suspension is fundamental in moderating the gamble of esophageal disease.

Influence on Generally Mortality:

The immediate wellbeing outcomes of smoking, enveloping respiratory illnesses and disease, add to a significant expansion in generally mortality among smokers.

Unexpected passing:

Smokers face a fundamentally higher gamble of sudden passing contrasted with non-smokers. The mix of respiratory sicknesses and different types of disease adds to an abbreviated future for people who smoke. Smoking-related infections are a significant supporter of the worldwide weight of untimely mortality.

Decreased Future:

Studies have reliably shown that smoking is related with a diminished future. The combined effect of smoking-related infections, combined with an expanded gamble of cardiovascular illnesses and other unexpected issues, adds to a more limited life expectancy for people who keep on smoking.

Handed-down cigarette smoke and Mortality:

The wellbeing results of smoking are not restricted to the people who effectively smoke; handed-down cigarette smoke openness additionally presents critical dangers. Non-smokers presented to handed-down cigarette smoke are at an expanded gamble of creating respiratory sicknesses and certain diseases. The effect of handed-down cigarette smoke on in general mortality stresses the significance of establishing sans smoke conditions to safeguard non-smokers.

General Wellbeing Drives and Smoking Suspension:

General wellbeing drives pointed toward decreasing smoking pervasiveness and supporting smoking suspension assume a pivotal part in relieving the immediate wellbeing outcomes of smoking.

Hostile to Smoking Efforts:

General wellbeing efforts zeroed in on bringing issues to light about the wellbeing dangers of smoking have been instrumental in teaching people in general. Realistic admonition marks on cigarette bundles, TV and on-line commercials, and local area based drives add to changing accepted practices and perspectives toward smoking.

Tobacco Control Strategies:

Tough tobacco control strategies are fundamental in checking the tobacco pandemic. These strategies incorporate promoting limitations, sans smoke regulations, expanded charges on tobacco items, and realistic admonition names. The execution and implementation of these approaches add to decreasing smoking predominance and forestalling inception.

Smoking Discontinuance Projects:

Smoking end programs offer help and assets to people hoping to stop smoking. These projects might incorporate guiding, nicotine substitution treatments (NRTs), doctor prescribed drugs, and innovation based mediations. Empowering and working with smoking suspension is an essential focal point of general wellbeing endeavors to relieve the wellbeing outcomes of smoking.

Youth Anticipation Drives:

Forestalling the inception of smoking among youth is a vital part of general wellbeing drives. School-based programs, local area commitment, and limitations on promoting to youth add to decreasing the commonness of smoking among more youthful populaces. Focusing on the variables that impact youth commencement is vital in molding future smoking patterns.

The immediate wellbeing results of smoking, including respiratory infections and disease, highlight the earnestness of thorough tobacco control endeavors. From the staggering effect of constant obstructive pneumonic infection (COPD) to the bleak truth of cellular breakdown in the lungs, the cost of smoking on individual wellbeing is enormous.

General wellbeing drives, administrative measures, and smoking suspension programs are fundamental parts of a multi-layered way to deal with combatting the tobacco pandemic. As the worldwide local area keeps on facing the difficulties presented by smoking-related sicknesses, continuous exploration, support, and a pledge to prove based mediations are crucial in accomplishing a future where the immediate wellbeing outcomes of smoking are limited, and social orders can flourish liberated from the weight of tobacco-related dismalness and mortality.

6.2 Discuss secondhand smoke and the impact of smoking on overall public health.

Examining handed-down cigarette smoke and the effect of smoking on by and large general wellbeing uncovers a perplexing interaction between individual ways of behaving, local area prosperity, and more extensive cultural ramifications. Handed-down cigarette smoke, otherwise called uninvolved smoke or natural tobacco smoke (ETS), presents huge wellbeing dangers to non-smokers, adding to a scope of unfavorable results. Besides, the commonness of smoking and openness to handed-down cigarette smoke have sweeping ramifications for general wellbeing, putting a significant weight on medical care frameworks, economies, and cultural prosperity.

Handed-down cigarette smoke and Wellbeing Dangers:

Handed-down cigarette smoke is a combination of the smoke discharged from the copying end of a cigarette, stogie, or line and the smoke breathed out by the smoker. It contains more than 7,000 synthetic substances, including hundreds that are harmful and around 70 known to cause malignant growth. The wellbeing gambles related with handed-down cigarette smoke openness are indisputably factual and reach out across different segment gatherings.

Respiratory Impacts:

Non-smokers presented to handed-down cigarette smoke are at an expanded gamble of respiratory issues, including hacking, wheezing, and fuel of asthma side effects. Kids presented to handed-down cigarette smoke are especially powerless, with a higher frequency of respiratory diseases, ear contaminations, and unexpected baby passing condition (SIDS). The aggravations and poisons in handed-down cigarette smoke can think twice about wellbeing, prompting constant circumstances like bronchitis and pneumonia.

Cardiovascular Results:

Handed-down cigarette smoke openness has huge cardiovascular ramifications, adding to an expanded gamble of coronary illness and stroke in non-smokers. The unsafe substances in handed-down cigarette smoke can prompt the choking of veins, increment circulatory strain, and advance the improvement of atherosclerosis. These cardiovascular impacts highlight the foundational effect of handed-down cigarette smoke on non-smokers' wellbeing.

Disease Hazard:

The cancer-causing agents present in handed-down cigarette smoke make non-smokers presented to it more helpless to specific malignant growths. While the gamble is lower than for dynamic smokers, long haul openness to handed-down cigarette smoke has been connected to an expanded frequency of cellular breakdown in the lungs, particularly among non-smoking mates of smokers. Moreover, openness to handed-down cigarette smoke during youth might raise the endanger of creating disease further down the road.

Unfavorable Pregnancy Results:

Pregnant ladies presented to handed-down cigarette smoke face a raised gamble of unfavorable pregnancy results, including low birth weight, pre-term birth, and formative issues. The poisons in handed-down cigarette smoke can cross the placenta, influencing fetal turn of events and adding to confusions during pregnancy. Shielding pregnant ladies from handed-down cigarette smoke is vital for maternal and youngster wellbeing.

Influence on Kids' Wellbeing:

Kids are especially powerless against the wellbeing impacts of handed-down cigarette smoke. Openness during adolescence is related with respiratory diseases, expanded asthma seriousness, and disabled lung improvement. Besides, handed-down cigarette smoke openness in youth can make way for a long lasting weakness to respiratory sicknesses and other wellbeing challenges.

Cultural Effect of Smoking on General Wellbeing:

The pervasiveness of smoking and openness to handed-down cigarette smoke contribute essentially to more extensive general wellbeing challenges, influencing populaces at the local area and cultural levels.

Medical services Framework Weight:

The medical services framework bears a significant weight because of the wellbeing outcomes of smoking and handed-down cigarette smoke openness. The therapy of smoking-related infections, including respiratory circumstances, cardiovascular illnesses, and disease, overwhelms medical services assets. The monetary expenses related with clinical consideration, hospitalizations, and drug mediations for smoking-related

ailments add to the generally speaking monetary weight on medical services frameworks.

Monetary Outcomes:

Smoking-related ailments and the related medical services costs have
financial repercussions at the cultural level. Lost efficiency because of
sickness, incapacity, and sudden passing among smokers and those presented to handed-down cigarette smoke adds to the monetary weight.
Also, the expenses of executing general wellbeing efforts, smoking discontinuance programs, and administrative measures to check smoking
add to the by and large financial effect.

Wellbeing Inconsistencies:

Smoking and handed-down cigarette smoke openness add to wellbeing
inconsistencies, excessively influencing weak populaces. Financial elements, including pay and instruction levels, frequently impact smoking
predominance and openness to handed-down cigarette smoke. Networks
with lower financial status might confront higher paces of smoking,
worsening existing wellbeing disparities.

Local area Prosperity:

The pervasiveness of smoking can affect local area prosperity by
impacting accepted practices and the actual climate. Networks with high
smoking rates might encounter reduced air quality because of expanded
handed-down cigarette smoke openness. Also, smoking-related litter, for
example, cigarette butts, adds to natural contamination, influencing the
general style and neatness of public spaces.

Stress on Friendly Administrations:

Smoking-related medical problems can overburden social administrations, including handicap backing and recovery administrations. People
experiencing smoking-related sicknesses might require continuous consideration and help, further burdening social emotionally supportive
networks. This strain highlights the requirement for thorough tobacco
control measures to mitigate the cultural weight related with smoking.

General Wellbeing Drives and Smoking Suspension:

Endeavors to address the effect of smoking on by and large general wellbeing include a diverse methodology, including general wellbeing drives,
administrative measures, and smoking suspension programs.

General Wellbeing Efforts:

General wellbeing efforts assume an essential part in bringing issues to
light about the wellbeing dangers of smoking and handed-down cigarette
smoke openness. Instructive drives, including broad communications crusades, local area effort, and school-based programs, expect to change accepted practices and perspectives towards smoking. Realistic admonition

marks on cigarette bundles are a visual hindrance, building up the well-being results of tobacco use.

Tobacco Control Arrangements:

Rigid tobacco control arrangements are fundamental in lessening smoking pervasiveness and safeguarding non-smokers from handed-down cigarette smoke. Approaches incorporate sans smoke regulations, limitations on tobacco publicizing and showcasing, expanded charges on tobacco items, and realistic admonition marks. The execution and requirement of these approaches add to establishing conditions that deter smoking and limit openness to handed-down cigarette smoke.

Smoking End Projects:

Smoking end programs offer help for people hoping to stop smoking. These projects might incorporate advising, nicotine substitution treatments (NRTs), physician recommended drugs, and innovation based intercessions. The objective is to engage people to defeat nicotine compulsion and decrease the commonness of smoking, in this manner limiting the effect of smoking on general wellbeing.

Local area Commitment and Support:

Local area commitment and support are fundamental parts of effective tobacco control drives. Engaging people group to advocate for sans smoke conditions, partake in enemy of tobacco missions, and backing strategy changes upgrades the viability of general wellbeing endeavors. Grassroots developments and local area driven drives add to switching accepted practices up smoking.

Youth Counteraction Drives:

Forestalling the commencement of smoking among youth is a vital focal point of general wellbeing drives. School-based programs, local area commitment, and limitations on advertising to youth add to decreasing the predominance of smoking among more youthful populaces. Focusing on the elements that impact youth commencement is urgent in molding future smoking patterns.

Worldwide Viewpoints and Difficulties:

The effect of smoking on by and large general wellbeing reaches out past individual nations, with worldwide ramifications and difficulties.

Worldwide Weight of Sickness:

Smoking contributes altogether to the worldwide weight of illness, with a great many passings yearly credited to tobacco use. The World Wellbeing Association (WHO) gauges that tobacco-related diseases represent in excess of 8 million passings every year, with the larger part happening in low-and center pay nations. The globalization of the tobacco business and the promoting of tobacco items to new populaces add to the industriousness of the worldwide tobacco plague.

Global Participation:

Tending to the effect of smoking on general wellbeing requires global participation and coordinated effort. Worldwide drives, for example, the System Show on Tobacco Control (FCTC) laid out by the WHO, give a structure to nations to cooperate in executing powerful tobacco control measures. Sharing prescribed procedures, research discoveries, and planning endeavors on a worldwide scale are fundamental in handling the difficulties presented by smoking.

Arising Patterns and Items:

The scene of tobacco use is developing with the rise of new items, including electronic cigarettes (e-cigarettes) and warmed tobacco items. These items acquaint new difficulties with tobacco control endeavors, with worries about their drawn out wellbeing impacts, appeal to youth, and expected influence on smoking pervasiveness. Tending to arising patterns requires nonstop examination, observing, and variation of administrative measures.

The conversation of handed-down cigarette smoke and the effect of smoking on generally general wellbeing underlines the requirement for far reaching and composed endeavors to address the perplexing difficulties presented by tobacco use.

From the wellbeing gambles looked by non-smokers presented to handed-down cigarette smoke to the more extensive cultural ramifications, the results of smoking reach out a long ways past individual decisions.

General wellbeing drives, administrative measures, and smoking discontinuance programs are critical in relieving the effect of smoking on general wellbeing. Worldwide collaboration, local area commitment, and imaginative methodologies are fundamental in adjusting to arising patterns and tending to the diligent difficulties presented by the tobacco plague.

A definitive objective is to establish conditions that advance wellbeing, decrease smoking predominance, and defend non-smokers from the hindering impacts of handed-down cigarette smoke, cultivating a future where social orders can flourish liberated from the weight of tobacco-related horribleness and mortality.

Chapter 7

Quitting the Habit

Stopping the propensity for smoking is a groundbreaking excursion that works on individual wellbeing as well as adds to more extensive general wellbeing objectives. The choice to stop smoking is a significant responsibility with extensive ramifications for actual prosperity, psychological wellness, and in general personal satisfaction. This investigation digs into the difficulties of nicotine compulsion, the diverse parts of smoking end, and the different systems and assets accessible to help people in their mission to stop the propensity and carry on with better existences.

Figuring out Nicotine Compulsion:

Stopping smoking is intrinsically difficult because of the habit-forming nature of nicotine, the essential psychoactive substance in tobacco. Nicotine enslavement includes complex connections in the cerebrum's prize framework, prompting physical and mental reliance. Perceiving the elements that add to nicotine enslavement is critical for people trying to end liberated from the propensity.

Nicotine and the Cerebrum:

Upon inward breath, nicotine quickly crosses the blood-cerebrum hindrance and ties to nicotinic acetylcholine receptors, setting off the arrival of synapses like dopamine. This delivery causes pleasurable situations and supports the craving to smoke. Over the long haul, the cerebrum adjusts to standard nicotine openness, prompting resistance and the requirement for expanded nicotine admission to accomplish similar impacts.

Mental Reliance:

Nicotine fixation reaches out past actual reliance to incorporate mental variables. Smoking becomes interwoven with day to day schedules, feelings, and social circumstances, making solid affiliations that add to desires. The formal parts of smoking, like lighting a cigarette after a dinner or throughout a break, support the mental reliance on the propensity.

Withdrawal Side effects:

Endeavors to stop smoking frequently bring about withdrawal side effects, further confusing the stopping system. Withdrawal side effects might incorporate touchiness, uneasiness, trouble concentrating, expanded hunger, and deep desires for nicotine. These side effects can be upsetting, making it provoking for people to keep up with their obligation to stopping.

The Multi-layered Excursion of Smoking Discontinuance:

Stopping smoking is a multi-layered venture that includes tending to both the physical and mental parts of compulsion. Fruitful smoking discontinuance requires a comprehensive methodology that thinks about individual inspirations, survival techniques, and the production of a strong climate.

Inspiration and Preparation to Stop:

Integral to the excursion of smoking end is the singular's inspiration and availability to stop. Inspiration can be characteristic, coming from a craving for further developed wellbeing, monetary investment funds, or the prosperity of friends and family. Outside factors, for example, wellbeing panics or prevalent difficulty, can likewise assume a part. Understanding individual inspirations gives an establishment to fostering a modified quit plan.

Setting a Quit Date:

Laying out a quit date is an unmistakable move toward the smoking discontinuance venture. Picking a particular date gives a reasonable objective and permits people to plan for the progress intellectually. The quit date denotes the start of a sans smoke life and fills in as a point of convergence for executing techniques to oversee desires and withdrawal side effects.

Establishing a Strong Climate:

A strong climate fundamentally impacts the outcome of smoking suspension endeavors. Drawing in with companions, family, or care groups can give support, understanding, and responsibility. Making a sans smoke home and work environment further builds up the obligation to stopping. Strong conditions limit triggers and upgrade the probability of supported achievement.

Methods for dealing with hardship or stress:

Creating compelling methods for dealing with stress is fundamental for exploring the difficulties of smoking discontinuance. Stress, weariness, and profound triggers are normal factors that add to backslide. Distinguishing elective survival techniques, like activity, care, or side interests, assists people with overseeing stressors without turning to smoking. Mental social procedures can likewise be significant in changing idea designs related with smoking.

Proficient Help:

Looking for proficient help can altogether improve the possibilities of effective smoking discontinuance. Medical care suppliers, including specialists, attendants, and advisors, can offer customized direction, recommend drugs to help with stopping, and screen progress. Nicotine substitution treatments (NRTs), like patches, gum, and tablets, give a controlled method for overseeing nicotine withdrawal.

Techniques and Assets for Stopping:

Stopping smoking is a profoundly individualized process, and different techniques and assets are accessible to help people on their excursion toward a without smoke life.

Nicotine Substitution Treatments (NRTs):

NRTs are intended to mitigate withdrawal side effects by giving controlled dosages of nicotine without the hurtful synthetic substances found in tobacco smoke. Patches, gum, tablets, nasal showers, and inhalers are normal types of NRTs. These items can be utilized as a component of a thorough quit plan and are available without a prescription or by solution.

Physician endorsed Meds:

A few physician endorsed meds are supported to help with smoking end. Bupropion (Zyban) and varenicline (Chantix) are drugs that work on synapse frameworks to diminish desires and withdrawal side effects. These drugs are normally endorsed after a careful evaluation by a medical services supplier.

Social Treatment:

Social treatment centers around distinguishing and changing the ways of behaving related with smoking. This approach assists people with creating adapting abilities, put forth objectives, and explore triggers that might prompt backslide. Individual guiding, bunch treatment, and phone quitlines are types of conduct support that can be vital to the stopping system.

Versatile Applications and Online Projects:

Progressions in innovation have prompted the improvement of versatile applications and online projects explicitly intended to help smoking suspension. These devices frequently incorporate highlights, for example, objective following, progress observing, and inspirational substance. They offer open and advantageous help for people looking to stop.

Support Gatherings and Advising:

Joining support gatherings or looking for guiding gives a feeling of local area and shared insight. Bunch meetings, whether face to face or virtual, permit people to interface with other people who are on a comparable excursion. Directing, whether individual or gathering based, offers an organized and steady climate for tending to the mental parts of enslavement.

Care and Stress-Decrease Procedures:

Integrating care and stress-decrease methods into day to day existence can improve flexibility during the stopping system. Practices like contemplation, profound breathing activities, and yoga add to unwinding and give solid options in contrast to smoking for the purpose of overseeing pressure.

Defeating Difficulties and Backslide Counteraction:

While the way to stopping smoking is loaded up with difficulties, backslide avoidance procedures are pivotal for keeping up with long haul achievement.

Recognizing Triggers and High-Chance Circumstances:

Understanding triggers that expeditious the longing to smoke is vital to backslide anticipation. Distinguishing high-risk circumstances, for example, get-togethers where others are smoking or snapshots of elevated pressure, permits people to proactively plan elective methods for dealing with hardship or stress.

Gaining from Misfortunes:

It's vital for view misfortunes as any open doors for advancing as opposed to as disappointments. Assuming that a backslide happens, people can ponder the variables that added to the slip by and change their quit plan in like manner. Gaining from difficulties fortifies versatility and improves the probability of supported achievement.

Changing Quit Plans:

Adaptability is essential in the stopping system. Assuming that underlying techniques demonstrate ineffectual, people can change their quit designs and investigate elective methodologies. This could include attempting various meds, looking for extra help, or taking on new methods for dealing with hardship or stress. The capacity to adjust improves the possibilities of long haul achievement.

Observing Achievements:

Perceiving and commending achievements in the stopping venture supports positive way of behaving. Whether it's the principal day without a cigarette, multi week sans smoke, or coming to a critical time span, recognizing accomplishments helps inspiration and gives a feeling of achievement.

Long haul Backing:

Long haul support is indispensable for supporting smoking discontinuance achievement. Indeed, even after the underlying testing period, continuous help from companions, family, or care groups assists people with exploring the highs and lows of existence without going to cigarettes. Normal registrations with medical care suppliers and cooperation in upkeep programs add to supported achievement.

Influence on Wellbeing and Prosperity:

The choice to stop smoking affects wellbeing, impacting both physical and mental prosperity.

Prompt Wellbeing Enhancements:

Not long after stopping, the body starts to encounter positive changes. Carbon monoxide levels decline, permitting oxygen levels in the blood to get back to business as usual. Lung capability improves, and dissemination starts to upgrade. These quick upgrades set up for long haul medical advantages.

Diminished Hazard of Persistent Infections:

Stopping smoking fundamentally lessens the gamble of creating ongoing sicknesses related with tobacco use. The gamble of coronary illness, stroke, respiratory circumstances, and different malignant growths diminishes over the long haul. The more drawn out a singular remaining parts sans smoke, the more prominent the decrease in these wellbeing chances.

Worked on Respiratory Capability:

Lung capability further develops step by step subsequent to stopping smoking. Hacking and windedness decline, and the gamble of constant obstructive aspiratory sickness (COPD) and other respiratory circumstances reduces. The respiratory framework starts to fix itself, upgrading generally speaking lung wellbeing.

Upgraded Cardiovascular Wellbeing:

The cardiovascular advantages of stopping smoking are significant. As the gamble of blood clumps, respiratory failures, and strokes diminishes, in general cardiovascular wellbeing moves along. The heart turns out to be more proficient, and veins recapture adaptability, adding to a diminished gamble of cardiovascular illnesses.

Positive Effect on Psychological wellness:

Stopping smoking is related with beneficial outcomes on emotional well-being. While the underlying difficulties of withdrawal might prompt temperament vacillations, long haul end is connected to diminished tension and misery. Further developed mental prosperity adds to a general better personal satisfaction.

Tending to Social and Ecological Variables:

Stopping smoking reaches out past individual endeavors and includes addressing social and natural factors that add to tobacco use.

Establishing Without smoke Conditions:

Laying out and advancing without smoke conditions is necessary to supporting smoking end endeavors. Without smoke strategies in homes, working environments, and public spaces add to diminishing openness to handed-down cigarette smoke and make a strong air for people attempting to stop.

Local area Commitment and Backing:

Local area commitment and support assume a fundamental part in molding normal practices around tobacco use. Grassroots developments, mindfulness missions, and backing endeavors add to the formation of conditions that deter smoking and advance general wellbeing. Networks have the ability to impact approaches, support drives, and decrease the predominance of smoking.

Youth Counteraction Drives:

Forestalling the commencement of smoking among youth is a proactive way to deal with lessening the general predominance of smoking. School-based programs, local area commitment, and limitations on promoting to youth add to forming mentalities toward smoking since the beginning.

Stopping the propensity for smoking is an extraordinary excursion that envelops physical, mental, and cultural aspects. Figuring out the difficulties of nicotine compulsion, embracing a complex way to deal with smoking suspension, and getting to different systems and assets are vital stages in making and keeping up with progress.

The choice to stop smoking has expansive ramifications for wellbeing, prosperity, and generally speaking personal satisfaction. Prompt wellbeing enhancements, decreased hazard of persistent illnesses, and beneficial outcomes on psychological well-being highlight the significant effect of stopping. Past individual endeavors, tending to social and natural variables, making steady networks, and taking part in backing add to an aggregate way to deal with lessening the worldwide weight of tobacco use.

As people leave on the excursion to stop smoking, the acknowledgment that stopping is a cycle, not an occasion, enables them to conquer difficulties, gain from misfortunes, and celebrate achievements. With continuous help, strength, and a guarantee to a sans smoke life, people can embrace a better future, adding to the more extensive objectives of general wellbeing and prosperity.

7.1 Explore the various methods and challenges of quitting smoking.

Investigating the different techniques and difficulties of stopping smoking digs into the intricacies of beating nicotine habit and the assorted procedures people utilize to make long haul progress. This investigation includes the scope of discontinuance techniques, the physiological and mental obstacles looked by people endeavoring to stop, and the advancing scene of smoking suspension draws near.

Stopping smoking is a diverse undertaking that requires a mix of responsibility, support, and successful methodologies. The habit-forming nature of nicotine, combined with the mental affiliations framed with smoking, presents critical difficulties for those looking to end liberated from the propensity. Nonetheless, different techniques and assets are accessible to help people in their excursion toward a sans smoke life.

The Nicotine Enslavement Challenge:

Vital to the test of stopping smoking is nicotine enslavement, which applies both physiological and mental impacts on people.

Nicotine's Effect on the Mind:

Nicotine, the essential psychoactive part in tobacco, ties to nicotinic acetylcholine receptors in the mind, prompting the arrival of synapses like dopamine. This cycle makes a feeling of joy and builds up the propensity for smoking. Over the long haul, the cerebrum adjusts to ordinary nicotine openness, prompting reliance and the requirement for expanded nicotine admission to keep up with the ideal impacts.

Mental Affiliations:

Past the physiological reliance, smoking becomes interwoven with different parts of day to day existence, framing solid mental affiliations. Smoking might be connected to schedules, feelings, social exercises, or stress alleviation. Breaking these affiliations is a pivotal part of stopping smoking and requires tending to both the physical and mental elements of enslavement.

Withdrawal Side effects:

At the point when people endeavor to stop smoking, they frequently experience withdrawal side effects as their bodies acclimate to the shortfall of nicotine. Normal withdrawal side effects incorporate peevishness, nervousness, trouble concentrating, expanded hunger, and deep desires for cigarettes. These side effects add to the difficulties of stopping and may prompt backslide while perhaps not actually made due.

Suspension Techniques and Methodologies:

Various techniques and methodologies are accessible to help people in their mission to stop smoking. These methodologies range from conduct intercessions to pharmacological guides and envelop both customary and inventive procedures.

Social Treatment:

Social treatment is a foundation of smoking suspension endeavors. This approach centers around recognizing and changing the ways of behaving related with smoking. Mental social treatment (CBT) is a generally utilized type of conduct treatment that helps people perceive and change thought examples and ways of behaving connected with smoking. Social intercessions might incorporate setting a quit date, creating ways of dealing with hardship or stress, and addressing triggers that add to smoking.

Nicotine Substitution Treatment (NRT):

Nicotine substitution treatment (NRT) furnishes people with a controlled portion of nicotine to ease withdrawal side effects and desires. Normal types of NRT incorporate nicotine patches, gum, capsules, nasal splashes, and inhalers. NRT permits people to bit by bit lessen their reliance on nicotine without openness to the hurtful synthetic substances in tobacco smoke. These items are available without a prescription or by remedy.

Physician endorsed Drugs:

A few physician endorsed drugs are supported to help with smoking suspension. Bupropion (Zyban) and varenicline (Chantix) are meds that work on synapse frameworks to decrease desires and withdrawal side effects. These prescriptions are commonly recommended after an intensive evaluation by a medical care supplier and might be utilized as a feature of a thorough quit plan.

Portable Applications and Online Projects:

Progressions in innovation have prompted the advancement of portable applications and online projects explicitly intended to help smoking discontinuance. These instruments frequently incorporate elements, for example, objective following, progress observing, and persuasive substance. Versatile applications and online projects offer open and advantageous help for people looking to stop and can be customized to fit individual necessities.

Care and Stress-Decrease Methods:

Integrating care and stress-decrease methods into smoking discontinuance endeavors can upgrade flexibility and advance long haul achievement. Practices like contemplation, profound breathing activities, and yoga add to unwinding and give solid options in contrast to smoking for of overseeing pressure.

Support Gatherings and Directing:

Support gatherings and directing assume a crucial part in the stopping system by giving a feeling of local area and shared insight. Bunch meetings, whether face to face or virtual, permit people to interface with other people who are on a comparable excursion. Directing, whether individual or gathering based, offers an organized and steady climate for tending to the mental parts of compulsion.

Hypnotherapy and Needle therapy:

Elective treatments, like hypnotherapy and needle therapy, are at times investigated as integral ways to deal with smoking suspension. While the proof supporting the viability of these techniques isn't quite as strong concerning different methodologies, a few people find benefit from the unwinding and stress decrease related with these practices.

Continuous Decrease and Pure and simple:

Stopping smoking can be moved toward either through continuous decrease or stopping "pure and simple." Steady decrease includes gradually diminishing the quantity of cigarettes smoked every day. While this approach might be more reasonable for certain people, it requires areas of strength for a to a definitive objective of stopping. Going "pure and simple" includes stopping suddenly without slow decrease. This strategy can be trying because of the unexpected suspension of nicotine, yet a few people lean toward this methodology for its conclusiveness.

Difficulties of Stopping:

Stopping smoking isn't without its difficulties, and people might experience different obstacles that can affect their progress in accomplishing long haul suspension.

Withdrawal Side effects and Desires:

Withdrawal side effects, including profound desires for nicotine, can be a huge test during the underlying periods of stopping. Desires might be set off by natural prompts, stress, or social circumstances. Dealing with these desires requires powerful survival methods and a solid obligation to the quit plan.

Mental Affiliations:

The mental affiliations shaped with smoking can continue even after the actual reliance on nicotine has reduced. People might find it trying to bring an end to the propensity for smoking in light of specific circumstances or feelings. Conduct treatment and care strategies are significant devices in tending to these mental affiliations.

Social and Natural Triggers:

Social and natural variables, for example, being around different smokers or visiting places related with smoking, can go about as triggers for backslide. Establishing a steady climate and creating procedures to explore these triggers are fundamental parts of a fruitful quit plan.

Feeling of dread toward Weight Gain:

The feeling of dread toward weight gain is a typical worry among people endeavoring to stop smoking. Nicotine has hunger suppressant impacts, and stopping might prompt expanded food admission and changes in digestion. Tending to this worry includes integrating good dieting propensities and standard active work into the quit plan.

Double Propensities (Smoking and Different Ways of behaving):

Smoking might be firmly connected to different ways of behaving, like drinking espresso, polishing off liquor, or enjoying reprieves at work. Ending these double propensities might expect acclimations to schedules and the improvement of elective exercises that don't include smoking.

Hesitance to Look for Proficient Assistance:

A few people might be hesitant to look for proficient assistance, either because of shame or a conviction that they can stop all alone. Notwithstanding, medical services suppliers assume a urgent part in giving direction, recommending meds, and observing advancement. Beating this hesitance can fundamentally improve the possibilities of fruitful end.

Developments in Smoking Suspension:

The scene of smoking suspension is consistently developing, with progressing examination and advancements presenting new methodologies and innovations.

E-Cigarettes and Vaping:

Electronic cigarettes (e-cigarettes) and vaping stand out as potential damage decrease apparatuses, yet their security and viability in smoking end remain subjects of discussion. While certain people have effectively utilized e-cigarettes to stop smoking, concerns exist in regards to the drawn out wellbeing impacts and the potential for youth commencement.

Telemedicine and Computerized Therapeutics:

The ascent of telemedicine and computerized therapeutics has extended admittance to smoking discontinuance support. Virtual advising meetings, online conduct treatment projects, and remote checking offer people adaptability and accommodation in getting proficient direction and backing.

Hereditary and Customized Approaches:

Research in hereditary qualities has opened roads for customized smoking suspension draws near. Understanding hereditary variables that impact a singular's reaction to nicotine and their probability of stopping effectively may prompt more customized mediations.

Mix Treatments:

Consolidating different discontinuance strategies, like matching social treatment with prescription or utilizing numerous kinds of NRT all the while, is an arising approach. This methodology intends to address both the physiological and mental parts of compulsion for a more far reaching treatment.

Investigating the different techniques and difficulties of stopping smoking highlights the intricacy of nicotine fixation and the assorted systems accessible to people trying to stop. From conduct intercessions to pharmacological guides, and from conventional techniques to inventive methodologies, the range of end choices considers customized quit plans custom-made to individual requirements.

While difficulties like withdrawal side effects, mental affiliations, and social triggers might present obstacles, the advancing scene of smoking end keeps on offering new apparatuses and bits of knowledge. Consolidating a mix of approaches, looking for proficient direction, and remaining focused on the quit plan are fundamental components in defeating these difficulties and accomplishing effective, long haul smoking end.

As the field of smoking end research advances, a more profound comprehension of the hereditary, social, and ecological variables impacting smoking ways of behaving will probably add to additional viable and customized mediations. At last, the excursion to stop smoking is extraordinary for every person, and the continuous obligation to a without smoke life is a groundbreaking and enabling decision with significant ramifications for wellbeing and prosperity.

7.2 Share personal stories of individuals who successfully kicked the habit.

The excursion of stopping smoking is much of the time set apart by private accounts of win, strength, and change. While the difficulties of beating nicotine dependence are huge, incalculable people have effectively phased out the vice, rousing others with their accounts of tirelessness and freshly discovered prosperity. These individual stories highlight the different ways to stopping and enlighten the close to home, physical, and mental changes that go with the choice to embrace a sans smoke life.

Story 1: Sarah's Excursion to Opportunity

Sarah, a 35-year-old showcasing proficient, set out on her excursion to stop smoking after a wellbeing alarm that left an enduring effect on her. Determined to have early indications of respiratory issues, Sarah knew that proceeding to smoke would risk her prosperity. With the backing of her family and a decided outlook, Sarah started her quit plan. She settled on a blend approach, coordinating social treatment meetings to address her smoking triggers and desires, and utilizing nicotine substitution treatment (NRT) to oversee withdrawal side effects.

Sarah stressed the significance of a strong climate, featuring how her family assumed a urgent part in her prosperity. Together, they took part in better exercises that supplanted the social parts of smoking. Ordinary registrations with a medical services supplier gave extra direction and support. Sarah's excursion displayed the extraordinary force of familial help, customized techniques, and a pledge to wellbeing.

Story 2: Imprint's Victory Over Double Addictions

Mark, a 45-year-old IT proficient, confronted the test of stopping smoking as well as conquering the double habit of smoking and unnecessary caffeine utilization. His process started when he understood that the interconnected idea of these propensities was obstructing his general prosperity. Mark picked a progressive decrease approach, gradually diminishing the two his cigarette admission and caffeine utilization.

To address the mental parts of his double addictions, Imprint integrated care procedures and standard activity into his everyday practice. These practices assisted him with overseeing pressure as well as given better options in contrast to his laid out propensities. Imprint's story featured the significance of perceiving and tending to interconnected ways of behaving, underscoring that effective stopping frequently includes an all encompassing methodology.

Story 3: Emily's Strength In the midst of Life Changes

Emily, a 28-year-old understudy, stood up to the test of stopping smoking during a time of huge life altering events. Adjusting scholarly tensions, work responsibilities, and individual difficulties, Emily ended up going to cigarettes as a method for dealing with hardship or stress. Perceiving the cost it was taking on her physical and psychological wellness, Emily concluded the time had come to break liberated from the cycle.

Her quit venture included enrolling the help of a smoking end instructor who directed her through the intricacies of overseeing pressure and adapting to life changes without depending on smoking. Emily additionally found the force of companion support through bunch treatment meetings, where she shared her encounters and gained from others confronting comparative battles. Emily's flexibility highlighted the significance of looking for proficient direction during wild life changes and the strength that can be drawn from shared encounters.

Story 4: James' Change Through Exercise

James, a 50-year-old development laborer, understood the negative effect of smoking on his actual perseverance and in general wellbeing. Not entirely settled to recover his imperativeness, James coordinated customary activity into his quit plan. He started with straightforward exercises like energetic strolls and step by step advanced to additional extreme exercises. The positive effect of activity on his lung limit and generally speaking prosperity turned into a strong inspiration in his excursion to stop smoking.

James featured how active work filled in as a double reason methodology - besides the fact that it occupied him from desires, yet it likewise added to his general wellbeing improvement. His story exemplified the cooperative connection between taking on a better way of life and conquering the difficulties of smoking suspension.

Story 5: Maria's Obligation to Parenthood

Maria, a 32-year-old eager mother, left on her quit venture spurred by the craving to give a solid climate to her unborn youngster. Perceiving the dangers related with smoking during pregnancy, Maria looked for direction from pre-birth care suppliers and signed up for a particular smoking end program for pregnant ladies. She tracked down comfort in associating with other hopeful moms confronting comparative difficulties.

Maria's obligation to her youngster's prosperity gave a strong main impetus to stop smoking. With the backing of her medical care group, Maria effectively explored the extraordinary difficulties related with smoking suspension during pregnancy, accentuating the significant effect of maternal assurance on the soundness of the future.

Story 6: David's Rehash Through Leisure activities

David, a 40-year-old visual planner, found the groundbreaking force of taking on new side interests as a component of his smoking suspension technique. Confronted with the ongoing idea of smoking during imaginative meetings, David chose to channel his energy into elective exercises. He investigated painting, photography, and carpentry as source for self-articulation.

Participating in these side interests not just occupied David from the longing to smoke yet additionally gave a feeling of achievement and satisfaction. Over the long run, the relationship among imagination and smoking was supplanted with better outlets, prompting an extensive change in his way of life and outlook.

Story 7: Linda's Excursion from Smoker to Backer

Linda, a 60-year-old retired person, vanquished her own smoking habit as well as turned into a supporter for smoking end locally. Her process started when a dear companion surrendered to smoking-related sicknesses, inciting Linda to rethink her own propensities. Not entirely settled to respect her companion's memory, she turned out to be effectively associated with neighborhood against smoking efforts.

Linda's story exhibited the significant effect that individual misfortune and a pledge to local area prosperity can have on one's excursion to stop smoking. By transforming her experience into support, Linda changed her own life as well as added to a more extensive development for general wellbeing.

These individual stories enlighten the assorted ways people take to stop smoking effectively. Every story mirrors an extraordinary blend of techniques, difficulties, and wellsprings of motivation, stressing that there is nobody size-fits-all way to deal with smoking end. From family backing and expert direction to way of life changes and promotion, these accounts feature the complex idea of the quit venture and the strength still up in the air to break liberated from the grasp of nicotine fixation.

These accounts likewise highlight the significance of perceiving that stopping is a powerful interaction, frequently set apart by misfortunes and wins. The common encounters of these people give trust, consolation, and significant experiences for others leaving on their own excursions to a without smoke life. As the aggregate voice of fruitful losers develops, so does the possibility to move support those actually exploring the difficulties of stopping smoking.

Chapter 8

The Global Tobacco Epidemic

The Worldwide Tobacco Pestilence: Unwinding the Complicated Trap of Difficulties and Arrangements
The worldwide tobacco pestilence addresses one of the main general wellbeing difficulties within recent memory. With establishes profoundly implanted ever, tobacco use has developed into an unavoidable and complex issue influencing a large number of lives around the world. This investigation dives into the diverse elements of the worldwide tobacco plague, inspecting its verifiable setting, current status, the effect on wellbeing and economies, and the continuous endeavors to check its predominance.

1. Verifiable Underlying foundations of Tobacco Use:
   Tobacco's process started hundreds of years prior, entwined with social, financial, and social turns of events. Native people groups in the Americas developed and involved tobacco for stylized and restorative purposes well before the appearance of European travelers. The boundless reception of tobacco in Europe and its ensuing worldwide spread denoted the beginning of an industry that would shape economies and impact social orders.

2. The Ascent of Business Tobacco:
   The progress from conventional tobacco use to business creation and utilization denoted a vital second in the tobacco story. The creation of the cigarette moving machine in the late nineteenth century changed the business, making large scale manufacturing plausible. This development, combined with forceful promoting techniques, prompted the flood in cigarette utilization during the twentieth hundred years.

3. **Worldwide Wellbeing Effect:**
The cost of the worldwide tobacco plague on general wellbeing is faltering. Smoking is a main source of preventable passings, adding to a heap of medical problems, including cardiovascular infections, respiratory issues, and different diseases. The World Wellbeing Association (WHO) appraises that tobacco use kills in excess of 8 million individuals yearly, with more than 7 million passings ascribed to coordinate tobacco use and around 1.2 million to handed-down cigarette smoke openness.

4. **Monetary Ramifications:**
While the tobacco business produces significant benefits, the financial outcomes of the worldwide tobacco plague are significant. Medical services consumptions connected with tobacco-related ailments strain medical care frameworks, influencing both created and emerging countries. Furthermore, the deficiency of efficiency because of sickness and untimely mortality intensifies the financial weight on social orders, making a complicated interaction between monetary interests and general wellbeing.

5. **Focusing on Weak Populaces:**
The tobacco business has a past filled with focusing on weak populaces, including youth, low-pay networks, and minimized gatherings. Forceful advertising efforts, enhanced items, and key situation of tobacco outlets add to the unbalanced effect on these networks. Understanding the financial determinants of tobacco use is vital for planning successful intercessions that address wellbeing incongruities.

6. **Administrative Measures and Peaceful accords:**
Perceiving the critical need to address the worldwide tobacco pestilence, the global local area has executed different administrative measures and arrangements. The System Show on Tobacco Control (FCTC), created by the WHO, addresses a milestone settlement pointed toward decreasing the interest for and supply of tobacco items.
Signatory nations focus on executing proof based tobacco control approaches, including measures connected with tax assessment, promoting, and bundling.

7. **Challenges in Execution:**
In spite of purposeful endeavors to battle the worldwide tobacco scourge, challenges persevere in the execution of powerful tobacco control measures. The tobacco business' all around financed campaigning endeavors, lawful difficulties, and strategies to subvert general wellbeing approaches present huge hindrances. Adjusting

monetary interests, political will, and general wellbeing goals requires continuous carefulness and coordinated effort.

8. Arising Patterns and Items:
The scene of tobacco use is advancing with the rise of new items, including electronic cigarettes (e-cigarettes) and warmed tobacco items. These items acquaint new difficulties with tobacco control endeavors, with worries about their drawn out wellbeing impacts, appeal to youth, and likely effect on smoking predominance. Tending to arising patterns requires ceaseless exploration, checking, and transformation of administrative measures.

9. The Job of Training and Mindfulness:
Training and mindfulness assume a pivotal part in handling the worldwide tobacco plague. Thorough general wellbeing efforts, school-based drives, and local area commitment endeavors add to changing cultural perspectives towards tobacco use. Engaging people with information about the wellbeing chances related with smoking and openness to handed-down cigarette smoke is principal in encouraging a without tobacco culture.

10. Worldwide Participation and Exploration:
The worldwide idea of the tobacco pestilence requires global participation and cooperative examination endeavors. Sharing prescribed procedures, directing multifaceted examinations, and understanding the different variables impacting tobacco use add to the advancement of powerful and setting explicit intercessions. Outfitting the force of worldwide associations is essential in tending to the transboundary challenges presented by tobacco.

11. The Crossing point with Non-Transferable Infections:
The worldwide tobacco plague converges with the rising weight of non-transmittable infections (NCDs), making an intensifying general wellbeing challenge. Tobacco use is a significant gamble factor for NCDs like cardiovascular infections, respiratory circumstances, and diseases. Incorporated approaches that address the interconnectedness of hazard elements and sicknesses are fundamental for exhaustive wellbeing advancement and infection counteraction.

12. The Effect on Feasible Turn of events:
The worldwide tobacco pandemic has suggestions for practical advancement objectives (SDGs), especially in the domains of wellbeing, financial success, and civil rights. Accomplishing SDGs connected with wellbeing and prosperity (SDG 3), neediness decrease (SDG 1), and social imbalances (SDG 10) requires a deliberate work to moderate the effect of tobacco use on weak populaces and advance

tobacco control measures as necessary parts of supportable turn of events.

13. The Eventual fate of Tobacco Control:

As the world wrestles with the multi-layered difficulties of the worldwide tobacco pandemic, the eventual fate of tobacco control relies on advancement, joint effort, and supported responsibility. Tackling mechanical progressions, utilizing information examination, and taking on proof based approaches will be significant in adjusting to arising patterns in tobacco utilization. Moreover, cultivating a culture of without tobacco conditions and enabling networks to advocate for their wellbeing will be fundamental in molding a sans smoke future.

The worldwide tobacco scourge remains as a complicated and constant test with extensive ramifications for general wellbeing, economies, and feasible turn of events. Resolving this complex issue requires a complete and cooperative methodology that traverses worldwide boundaries, includes different partners, and coordinates proof based techniques.

From the authentic underlying foundations of tobacco use to the development of new items and patterns, the account of the worldwide tobacco pandemic is ceaselessly advancing. While progress has been pursued through peaceful accords, administrative measures, and public mindfulness crusades, the continuous fight against the tobacco business' impact requires unfaltering responsibility.

As social orders explore the mind boggling snare of monetary interests, wellbeing incongruities, and advancing utilization designs, the significance of shared liability and aggregate activity couldn't possibly be more significant. The worldwide local area should keep on gaining from victories and difficulties, improve in tobacco control systems, and backer for strategies that focus on general wellbeing over benefit.

Chasing a tobacco-liberated world, the illustrations gained from the worldwide tobacco plague act as an aide for molding strategies, cultivating mindfulness, and enabling people and networks to break liberated from the hold of tobacco. Through supported endeavors, worldwide collaboration, and a pledge to focusing on wellbeing, the vision of a world liberated from the overwhelming effect of tobacco can turn into a reality.

8.1 Investigate the worldwide impact of tobacco use on different cultures and societies.

Exploring the Overall Effect of Tobacco Use on Various Societies and Social orders

Tobacco use, with its profound verifiable roots and broad pervasiveness, has made a permanent imprint on societies and social orders across the globe. This investigation digs into the multi-layered effect of tobacco use, taking into account its verifiable importance, social affiliations, wellbeing suggestions, and the shifted reactions of various social orders to this unavoidable propensity. From ceremonies and customs to the intricacies of dependence and the difficulties of tobacco control, the overall effect of tobacco use unfurls in an embroidery of social variety and shared wellbeing concerns.

1. **Verifiable Setting:**
   Tobacco's process started in the Americas, where native societies developed and involved it for stately and restorative purposes well before the appearance of European colonizers. The trading of tobacco between the Old and New Universes changed it into a worldwide product. The fuse of tobacco into different social practices, both stately and sporting, established the groundwork for its assorted use in social orders around the world.

2. **Social Affiliations and Ceremonies:**
   Tobacco has expected assorted social implications, becoming woven into the texture of customs, services, and social connections. In numerous native societies, tobacco assumes a sacrosanct part, representing an association with the profound domain and filling in as a contribution in services. Moreover, in different social orders, tobacco use is profoundly implanted in friendly traditions, like smoking lines during political gatherings or praising achievements with stogies. Understanding the social meaning of tobacco is vital for perceiving its effect on networks and molding powerful tobacco control techniques that regard social variety.

3. **Wellbeing Incongruities and Civil rights:**
   Tobacco use frequently compounds existing wellbeing abberations and social imbalances inside social orders. Weak populaces, incorporating those with lower financial status, may encounter higher paces of tobacco-related illnesses. The tobacco business' designated promoting and estimating systems add to the unbalanced weight of smoking on underestimated networks. Tending to these differences requires a nuanced approach that thinks about social setting, financial variables, and the interconnected idea of wellbeing and civil rights.

4. **Orientation Elements:**
   The effect of tobacco use stretches out to orientation elements inside social orders. Generally, tobacco use has been gendered, with explicit social standards administering who smokes and in what settings. In certain societies, smoking might be all the more socially

adequate for men, while ladies face criticism for taking part in a similar way of behaving. Understanding these orientation elements is urgent for carrying out powerful and socially delicate tobacco control strategies that record for assorted social jobs and assumptions.

5. Tobacco Industry Strategies:
The tobacco business, with its worldwide reach, utilizes shifted strategies to impact various societies and social orders. Promoting techniques, item advancements, and campaigning endeavors are custom-made to take advantage of social subtleties and avoid administrative measures. The business' effect on social impression of smoking and its capacity to shape accepted practices highlight the requirement for thorough, socially educated ways to deal with neutralize its effect.

6. Differed Reactions to Tobacco Control:
Cultural reactions to tobacco control endeavors differ broadly, impacted by social mentalities, political environments, and financial contemplations. A few social orders have embraced rigid tobacco control measures, including complete smoking boycotts, realistic admonition marks, and forceful enemy of smoking efforts. Conversely, others might confront moves in carrying out such measures because of social opposition, financial reliance on tobacco creation, or the strong impact of the tobacco business.

7. Challenges in Low-and Center Pay Nations:
Low-and center pay nations frequently stand up to extraordinary difficulties in tending to the effect of tobacco use. These difficulties might incorporate restricted assets for general wellbeing drives, the impact of global tobacco companies, and an absence of mindfulness about the drawn out wellbeing results of smoking. Fitting mediations to the social setting and teaming up with nearby networks are fundamental for conquering these difficulties and advancing supportable tobacco control.

8. Smokeless Tobacco and Social Practices:
Past smoking, the utilization of smokeless tobacco items is common in specific societies. Smokeless structures, like snuff, biting tobacco, or betel quid, are profoundly implanted in social practices in different districts. Understanding the wellbeing chances related with smokeless tobacco use and tending to its social importance is indispensable for planning compelling intercessions that regard social customs while advancing general wellbeing.

9. The Effect on Youth and Arising Grown-ups:
Tobacco's impact on youth and arising grown-ups is a worldwide concern, rising above social limits. The tobacco business frequently

targets more youthful socioeconomics through enhanced items, promoting efforts, and item advancements. Understanding the social factors that add to youth commencement and executing preventive measures customized to explicit social settings are fundamental for checking the tobacco plague among people in the future.

10. **Social Responsiveness in Tobacco Control Missions:**
Planning socially delicate tobacco control crusades is central for their viability. Crusades should think about social qualities, convictions, and correspondence styles to resound with different populaces. Socially customized messages that address the particular difficulties and inspirations inside various social orders can improve the effect of hostile to smoking drives.

11. **Native Points of view and Cooperative Methodologies:**
Native people group, with novel social viewpoints on tobacco, frequently face unmistakable difficulties in tending to smoking-related medical problems. Cooperative methodologies that regard native information, draw in local area pioneers, and consolidate conventional mending rehearses are fundamental for cultivating powerful tobacco control procedures that line up with social qualities.

12. **Worldwide Wellbeing Tact:**
Tending to the overall effect of tobacco use requires a cooperative and strategic methodology on the worldwide stage. Global endeavors, for example, the Structure Show on Tobacco Control (FCTC), represent the significance of shared liability in handling a typical wellbeing challenge. Developing worldwide wellbeing strategy energizes data trade, shared help, and the pooling of assets to propel far reaching tobacco control drives.

13. **Moving Social Accounts:**

As social orders develop, so do social accounts encompassing tobacco use. Moving mentalities towards smoking, driven by expanded consciousness of wellbeing gambles and changing normal practices, add to a worldwide development against tobacco. Grassroots drives, driven by people and networks, assume an imperative part in reshaping social stories and encouraging a without tobacco ethos.

Examining the overall effect of tobacco use on various societies and social orders uncovers a complicated exchange of verifiable heritages, social affiliations, and wellbeing inconsistencies. The worldwide tobacco pandemic is certainly not a one-size-fits-all test; rather, it requires nuanced, socially educated approaches that regard variety while tending to shared wellbeing concerns.

As social orders wrestle with the social, financial, and wellbeing ramifications of tobacco use, the requirement for complete, proof based tobacco control measures turns out to be progressively obvious. Recognizing the social meaning of tobacco inside various settings, cultivating worldwide cooperation, and enabling networks to drive change are vital parts of a purposeful work to ease the overall weight of the tobacco plague. In this aggregate undertaking, the objective isn't simply to battle smoking however to advance wellbeing, value, and social protection on a worldwide scale.

8.2 Discuss the efforts of international organizations to combat the global tobacco epidemic.

Examining the endeavors of global associations to battle the worldwide tobacco scourge divulges a multi-layered and cooperative methodology pointed toward tending to one of the main general wellbeing challenges around the world. Worldwide associations assume a critical part in organizing methodologies, cultivating worldwide collaboration, and supporting for strategies that advance tobacco control and lessen the commonness of smoking-related sicknesses. This investigation digs into the drives, arrangements, and mediations drove by unmistakable worldwide bodies in the continuous fight against the worldwide tobacco plague.

1. World Wellbeing Association (WHO) and the System Show on Tobacco Control (FCTC):

   The World Wellbeing Association (WHO) remains at the front of worldwide endeavors to battle the tobacco pandemic. The Structure Show on Tobacco Control (FCTC), laid out by the WHO in 2003, addresses a milestone global settlement intended to address the transboundary idea of tobacco use. The FCTC is a far reaching and proof based system that gives rules to carrying out compelling tobacco control strategies, covering regions like evaluating and tax collection, publicizing and advancement, without smoke conditions, and bundling and marking.

   The FCTC's Center Goals:

   The FCTC's center goals incorporate forestalling tobacco use commencement, advancing smoking discontinuance, safeguarding individuals from openness to tobacco smoke, managing tobacco item happy, controlling tobacco publicizing and advancement, and diminishing illegal exchange tobacco items. By laying out a normalized set of measures, the FCTC works with a bound together worldwide reaction to the difficulties presented by the tobacco business.

   Worldwide Effect of the FCTC:

   Since its reception, the FCTC has acquired inescapable global help, with 182 Gatherings (181 nations and the European Association) starting around 2022. The settlement's effect is clear in the execution of tobacco control arrangements across different social and monetary settings. Gatherings to the FCTC focus on embracing and executing proof based measures, giving an establishment to worldwide collaboration in the battle against tobacco.

2. Worldwide Coordination and Organizations:
Global associations expand their compass by encouraging cooperation among legislatures, non-administrative associations (NGOs), and different partners. The cooperative endeavors of these elements intensify the effect of tobacco control drives and add to the pooling of assets and ability.

The Job of WHO in Coordination:
The WHO, as the planning office for worldwide wellbeing matters, assumes a focal part in organizing global endeavors. It gives specialized help, works with information trade, and supports nations in executing tobacco control measures. The WHO's commitment reaches out to provincial workplaces and associations with other global bodies, fortifying the aggregate reaction to the tobacco pestilence.

Organizations with NGOs and Common Society:
Cooperative drives including global associations, state run administrations, and non-legislative associations are urgent in tending to the perplexing difficulties presented by the tobacco business. NGOs and common society associations contribute important viewpoints, grassroots activation, and backing endeavors that supplement crafted by global bodies. Organizations cultivate a more far reaching and comprehensive way to deal with tobacco control.

3. Observing and Reconnaissance:
To check the viability of tobacco control measures and track worldwide patterns, global associations participate in observing and observation endeavors. Gathering information on tobacco use pervasiveness, openness to handed-down cigarette smoke, and the effect of mediations considers proof based independent direction and the ID of regions requiring designated activity.

Worldwide Grown-up Tobacco Study (GATS):
The Worldwide Grown-up Tobacco Study (GATS), upheld by the WHO and the Habitats for Infectious prevention and Counteraction (CDC), is a critical instrument for evaluating tobacco use designs. Led in different nations, GATS gives normalized information on tobacco utilization, information, and mentalities, supporting policymakers in fitting mediations to explicit settings.

Tobacco Map book and Other Reconnaissance Instruments:

Distributions like the Tobacco Map book, created by the American Malignant growth Society and the World Lung Establishment, offer an exhaustive outline of the worldwide tobacco scene. These assets incorporate information on tobacco-related infections, financial effect, and strategy viability, giving a significant reference to policymakers, specialists, and supporters.

4. Support for Strategy Change:
Worldwide associations effectively advocate for strategy changes at the public and worldwide levels, utilizing their impact to advance proof based measures and counter industry impedance. Backing endeavors incorporate a scope of strategy spaces, from tax collection and promoting limitations to without smoke conditions and bundling guidelines.

Tobacco Tax collection Approaches:
Perceiving the job of cost in affecting tobacco utilization, worldwide associations advocate for powerful tax collection approaches. Higher expenses on tobacco items lessen reasonableness as well as produce income for wellbeing drives. The WHO's MPOWER bundle incorporates proposals for expanding tobacco charges, accentuating their effect on decreasing tobacco use.

Publicizing and Advancement Limitations:
Support against tobacco publicizing and advancement is a vital part of worldwide tobacco control. The FCTC suggests exhaustive restrictions on tobacco publicizing, advancement, and sponsorship. Worldwide associations work to bring issues to light about the tricky strategies utilized by the tobacco business and backing nations in carrying out severe promoting limitations.

Without smoke Conditions:
Establishing without smoke conditions is a center goal of tobacco control endeavors. Worldwide associations advocate for regulation that disallows smoking in broad daylight spaces, work environments, and indoor settings. The outcome of such strategies is clear in the decrease of handed-down cigarette smoke openness and the advancement of without smoke standards.

5. Tending to Arising Difficulties:
The tobacco scene persistently develops with the rise of new items and difficulties. Global associations adjust their methodologies to resolve arising issues, like electronic cigarettes (e-cigarettes) and warmed tobacco items.

E-Cigarettes and Warmed Tobacco Items:
The ascent of e-cigarettes and warmed tobacco items presents difficulties to conventional tobacco control endeavors. Worldwide

associations participate in research, strategy advancement, and backing to address the remarkable dangers related with these items. Offsetting hurt decrease potential with the counteraction of youth commencement is a critical thought in forming worldwide reactions.

Exploration and Rules:

Worldwide associations put resources into exploration to grasp the wellbeing ramifications of arising tobacco items. Rules and suggestions are created to direct nations in controlling these items really. Cooperative endeavors guarantee an organized reaction to the developing scene of tobacco utilization.

6. **Fighting Industry Obstruction:**

   The tobacco business, known for its forceful promoting strategies and endeavors to subvert general wellbeing strategies, stays an imposing rival in the worldwide battle against tobacco. Global associations effectively work to counter industry impedance and advance arrangements that focus on general wellbeing.

   Execution of Article 5.3 of the FCTC:

   Article 5.3 of the FCTC tends to the need to safeguard general wellbeing strategies from tobacco industry impedance. Global associations advocate for the severe execution of Article 5.3, asking legislatures to oppose industry pressure and keep up with independence in planning and carrying out tobacco control measures.

   Worldwide Tobacco Industry Checking:

   Checking the exercises of the tobacco business is a vital part of forestalling obstruction. Worldwide associations team up with states and common society to follow industry systems, uncover misleading practices, and reinforce administrative structures that protect general wellbeing strategies from unjustifiable impact.

7. **Financing and Asset Preparation:**

   Supported endeavors to battle the worldwide tobacco pandemic require monetary assets. Global associations assume a significant part in preparing reserves, supporting examination, and working with limit building drives to fortify public tobacco control programs.

   FCTC Execution Help:

   The WHO offers help to nations in executing the FCTC through specialized help, limit building, and financing potential open doors. This help assists nations with exploring the intricacies of tobacco control and guarantees that proof based measures are actually executed.

   Associations with Contributors and Magnanimous Associations:

   Joint efforts with contributors and altruistic associations add to the monetary supportability of tobacco control drives. Organizations work with the distribution of assets for examination, backing, and the execution of far reaching tobacco control approaches.

8. **Difficulties and Open doors:**
Regardless of critical advancement, challenges endure in the world-wide battle against tobacco. The tobacco business' versatility, industry impedance, and arising items present continuous difficulties. Nonetheless, the aggregate endeavors of global associations present open doors for conquering these difficulties through supported backing, examination, and cooperation.

Worldwide Financial Movements:
Monetary moves and economic accords can impact tobacco creation and utilization designs. Worldwide associations draw in with policy-makers to explore the intricacies of economic accords, guaranteeing that tobacco control measures are not compromised in that frame of mind of financial goals.

Cross-Sectoral Cooperation:
Perceiving the interconnected idea of wellbeing, exchange, and improvement, worldwide associations advance cross-sectoral coordinated effort. Drawing in with areas past wellbeing, like money and exchange, empowers a more all encompassing way to deal with tobacco control that thinks about different strategy spaces.

9. **Looking Forward: Future Headings in Worldwide Tobacco Control:**

The scene of worldwide tobacco control is dynamic, requiring non-stop transformation to arising difficulties and valuable open doors. The endeavors of worldwide associations will shape the future direction of tobacco control, stressing development, inclusivity, and a pledge to general wellbeing.

Advancement in Tobacco Control Methodologies:
The developing idea of the tobacco pandemic requests imaginative techniques. Global associations put resources into research on clever intercessions, tackling innovative progressions, and investigating conduct mediations to upgrade the adequacy of tobacco control measures.

Youth Commitment and Strengthening:
Perceiving the powerlessness of youth to tobacco commencement, global associations stress youth commitment and strengthening. Instructive drives, promotion missions, and local area based programs enable youngsters to become advocates for tobacco control, cultivating a generational change in mentalities towards smoking.

Tending to Wellbeing Disparities:

Worldwide associations focus on addressing wellbeing disparities connected with tobacco use. Fitting mediations to the necessities of weak populaces, tending to financial determinants, and upholding for strategies that decrease inconsistencies stay fundamental to the worldwide tobacco control plan.

Worldwide Promotion Organizations:

Expanding on the outcome of worldwide support organizations, global associations reinforce joint efforts with common society, NGOs, and local area pioneers. The force of aggregate backing and grassroots preparation is saddled to drive strategy change, counter industry impact, and elevate a common obligation to a tobacco-liberated world.

Environmental Change and Supportable Turn of events:

Perceiving the convergences between tobacco development, deforestation, and environmental change, worldwide associations incorporate tobacco control into more extensive maintainable advancement objectives. Methodologies that line up with ecological manageability add to a more exhaustive way to deal with worldwide wellbeing.

The endeavors of worldwide associations to battle the worldwide tobacco scourge embody an aggregate obligation to general wellbeing, value, and practical turn of events. Through drives, for example, the Structure Show on Tobacco Control, support for proof based strategies, and cooperative associations, these associations add to a worldwide development against tobacco use.

As the world explores the difficulties presented by the tobacco business, arising items, and the developing scene of general wellbeing, global associations stay at the front line of forming compelling reactions. The fate of worldwide tobacco control lies in proceeded with development, cross-sectoral cooperation, and an immovable commitment to the standards illustrated in peaceful accords. At last, the vision of a tobacco-liberated world relies upon the supported endeavors of legislatures, common society, and global associations working pair to defeat the worldwide tobacco plague.

Chapter 9

Innovations and Alternatives

Developments and Choices in Tobacco Control: Exploring a Sans smoke Future

The scene of tobacco control is advancing as social orders, wellbeing experts, and policymakers investigate advancements and choices to address the persevering difficulties presented by smoking. This investigation digs into the different cluster of advancements and options in the domain of tobacco control, from hurt decrease methodologies and mechanical developments to arising items and strategy mediations. By inspecting these turns of events, we gain experiences into the powerful endeavors pointed toward reshaping the story of tobacco use and imagining a without smoke future.

1. Hurt Decrease Systems:

   Prologue to Mischief Decrease:

   Hurt decrease procedures in tobacco control center around limiting the antagonistic wellbeing results related with smoking as opposed to upholding for complete restraint. While the idea has earned consideration lately, it stays a subject of discussion, with defenders featuring its possible advantages and pundits communicating worries about unseen side-effects.

   Electronic Cigarettes (E-cigarettes):

   E-cigarettes, or vaping gadgets, address an unmistakable damage decrease instrument that has acquired prevalence among smokers searching for options. These battery-fueled gadgets heat a fluid (frequently containing nicotine) to make a spray, giving a smoking-like encounter without the ignition of tobacco. Research on the drawn out wellbeing impacts of e-cigarettes is progressing, and questions continue about their security and potential for youth inception.

Heat-Not-Consume Tobacco Items:

Heat-not-consume tobacco items, for example, warmed tobacco sticks, offer an option in contrast to conventional smoking by warming as opposed to consuming tobacco. This interaction creates an inhalable spray containing nicotine. While these items might lessen openness to unsafe synthetics contrasted with conventional cigarettes, inquiries regarding their general security and potential wellbeing influences remain.

Snus and Smokeless Tobacco:

Smokeless tobacco items, including snus, have a long history and are frequently thought to be less unsafe than ignitable cigarettes. Snus, a kind of wet snuff, is well known in certain districts, especially in Scandinavia. While it conveys less dangers than smoking, concerns persevere about its habit-forming potential and wellbeing outcomes, stressing the requirement for thorough mischief decrease procedures.

2. **Mechanical Developments:**

Portable Applications and Computerized Stages:

Innovation assumes a critical part in supporting smoking end and advancing tobacco control. Portable applications and computerized stages give open assets, including customized quit plans, following apparatuses, and support networks. These advancements influence the omnipresence of cell phones to arrive at different populaces and upgrade the viability of end endeavors.

Web based Guiding and Telehealth Administrations:

Telehealth administrations, including web based guiding and virtual care groups, offer advantageous and open roads for people looking for help with stopping smoking. The capacity to associate with medical services experts remotely eliminates boundaries to get to, particularly for those in underserved or distant regions.

Enormous Information and Prescient Investigation:

Enormous information and prescient investigation add to a more profound comprehension of smoking examples, risk factors, and powerful mediations. By dissecting huge datasets, specialists and general wellbeing experts can distinguish patterns, target high-risk populaces, and designer mediations to people's particular necessities, improving the accuracy and effect of tobacco control endeavors.

3. **Arising Items and Exploration:**

Plant-Based Other options:

The investigation of plant-based options in contrast to conventional tobacco offers a clever way to deal with hurt decrease. Analysts are exploring plant-based details that emulate the tactile parts of smoking without the hurtful impacts of tobacco ignition. These options mean to give a fantastic encounter while limiting wellbeing chances.

Nicotine Substitution Treatments (NRTs):

Conventional nicotine substitution treatments, including patches, gum, tablets, and nasal showers, keep on being fundamental parts of smoking end endeavors. Continuous exploration investigates advancements in NRTs, like effective details and customized conveyance frameworks, to upgrade their adequacy and client experience.

Hereditary and Accuracy Medication Approaches:

Progresses in hereditary and accuracy medication empower a more designated way to deal with smoking end. Research investigates the hereditary variables affecting vulnerability to nicotine habit and reactions to suspension intercessions. Customized treatment plans in view of people's hereditary profiles hold guarantee for further developing discontinuance results.

4. Strategy Intercessions and Guideline:

Tobacco 21 and Age Limitations:

Strategy intercessions, like raising the legitimate age for buying tobacco items to 21 (Tobacco 21), intend to diminish youth inception. These actions recognize the weakness of youthful populaces to the habit-forming properties of nicotine and try to make boundaries to get to, in this way controling the commencement of tobacco use.

Plain Bundling and Realistic Wellbeing Alerts:

The execution of plain bundling and realistic wellbeing alerts on tobacco items is a strategy approach pointed toward diminishing the allure of smoking. By limiting marking and accentuating wellbeing gambles, these actions add to changing cultural impression of smoking and support quit endeavors.

Tobacco Charges and Value Systems:

Tobacco charges and cost systems stay powerful devices for lessening tobacco utilization. Greater costs beat smoking down, particularly among cost delicate populaces. Moreover, reserving charge incomes for tobacco control programs makes a manageable source of financial support for hostile to smoking drives.

5. Social and Mental Methodologies:

Care and Smoking Discontinuance:

Care based mediations definitely stand out enough to be noticed for their likely in smoking discontinuance. Care rehearses, for example, reflection and careful mindfulness, assist people with overseeing pressure, desires, and profound triggers related with smoking. Coordinating care into smoking end programs offers an all encompassing way to deal with breaking the pattern of habit.

Mental Social Treatment (CBT):

Mental social treatment stays a foundation of smoking end programs. CBT tends to the mental parts of smoking, helping people recognize and change thought processes and conduct related with tobacco use. Incorporating CBT into complete discontinuance intercessions improves the viability of stopping endeavors.

6. Difficulties and Contemplations:

Potentially negative results of Mischief Decrease:

While hurt decrease procedures expect to moderate wellbeing gambles, worries about potentially negative results persevere. These may incorporate the renormalization of smoking ways of behaving, potential entryway impacts for youth, and vulnerabilities about the drawn out wellbeing effects of arising items. Offsetting hurt decrease with general wellbeing objectives requires cautious thought.

Administrative Difficulties and Industry Strategies:

The tobacco business' versatility presents difficulties to administrative systems. The advancement of new items and strategies to bypass guidelines requires constant watchfulness. Reinforcing administrative instruments, observing industry exercises, and expecting future patterns are fundamental parts of powerful tobacco control.

Value and Admittance to Options:

Guaranteeing fair admittance to hurt decrease instruments and options is significant for their viability. Abberations in access, affected by financial elements and geographic area, may worsen wellbeing imbalances. Systems to advance inclusivity and address obstructions to get to are essential for the progress of damage decrease drives.

Far reaching Ways to deal with Tobacco Control:

Perceiving the perplexing idea of tobacco use, extensive methodologies that join hurt decrease, strategy intercessions, and social procedures are fundamental. Combination of proof based rehearses, persistent examination, and variation to arising difficulties add to a more nuanced and compelling tobacco control plan.

7. Future Bearings: Toward a Smoke-Liberated World:

The quest for a smoke-liberated world requires continuous development, joint effort, and a guarantee to prove based techniques. As the scene of tobacco control keeps on advancing, a few key contemplations shape the future direction of endeavors to diminish smoking predominance.

Youth Avoidance and Schooling:

Focusing on youth counteraction and instruction stays essential to accomplishing a sans smoke future. Extensive school-based programs, local area exceed, and designated crusades address the remarkable difficulties presented by the tobacco business' promoting strategies and forestall the inception of tobacco use among youngsters.

Worldwide Joint effort and Information Trade:

The worldwide idea of the tobacco plague highlights the significance of global joint effort. Information trade, sharing prescribed procedures, and adjusting techniques on a worldwide scale add to an aggregate exertion that rises above lines and addresses the interconnected difficulties of tobacco control.

Tending to Financial Determinants:

Perceiving the financial determinants of tobacco use, future endeavors ought to address hidden abberations. Fighting tobacco-related well-being disparities requires an exhaustive methodology that thinks about friendly, monetary, and ecological elements, meaning to make conditions that help without tobacco ways of life.

Local area Commitment and Strengthening:

Engaging people group to play a functioning job in tobacco control cultivates reasonable change. Local area drove drives, grassroots preparation, and the inclusion of different partners add to a feeling of pride and obligation, enhancing the effect of tobacco control endeavors.

Advancement in Exploration and Assessment:

Progressing examination and assessment endeavors are fundamental for remaining in front of arising patterns and refining tobacco control techniques. Advancement in research philosophies, information examination, and assessment structures upgrades the proof base, directing the improvement of compelling mediations and strategies.

Developments and choices in tobacco control address a unique reaction to the difficulties presented by smoking. From hurt decrease techniques and mechanical developments to strategy mediations and arising items, the different cluster of approaches mirrors a guarantee to reshaping the direction of tobacco use.

As social orders endeavor toward a without smoke future, the cooperative endeavors of people, networks, medical care experts, policymakers, and scientists will assume a significant part in understanding the vision of a world liberated from the staggering effects of tobacco.

9.1 Explore emerging technologies and alternative products designed to reduce harm.

Investigating Arising Advances and Elective Items Intended to Lessen Mischief in Tobacco Utilization

The scene of tobacco utilization is going through critical change with the development of novel advances and elective items pointed toward lessening hurt related with smoking. As social orders wrestle with the industrious wellbeing takes a chance with presented by conventional tobacco use, specialists, trailblazers, and general wellbeing advocates are investigating inventive answers for give smokers choices that limit hurt. This investigation digs into the domain of arising advances and elective items, analyzing their likely advantages, challenges, and the more extensive effect on general wellbeing.

1. Electronic Nicotine Conveyance Frameworks (Finishes):
   Prologue to Closures:
   Electronic Nicotine Conveyance Frameworks (Closures), normally known as e-cigarettes or vaping gadgets, address quite possibly of the most noticeable advancement in hurt decrease. Closes capability by warming a fluid (generally containing nicotine, flavorings, and different synthetic substances) to make a spray, which is then breathed in. This cycle plans to reproduce the tangible experience of smoking while at the same time disposing of the ignition of tobacco.
   Possible Advantages:
   Closes are frequently promoted for their potential damage decrease benefits. Dissimilar to customary cigarettes, Finishes don't include the burning of tobacco, lessening openness to destructive tar and various cancer-causing synthetic compounds related with smoking. A few smokers might track down Finishes a less hurtful option while as yet fulfilling their nicotine desires.
   Difficulties and Concerns:
   Regardless of possible advantages, concerns encompass the utilization of Finishes. The wellbeing of breathing in the airborne synthetic compounds in e-cigarettes is still being scrutinized, and long haul wellbeing impacts stay unsure. Also, the allure of seasoned e-cigarettes to youth has raised worries about the potential for expanded nicotine dependence among more youthful populaces.

2. Heat-Not-Consume (HNB) Tobacco Items:
   Prologue to HNB Items:
   Heat-Not-Consume (HNB) tobacco items address an elective way to deal with smoking that includes warming tobacco instead of consuming it. These items, for example, warmed tobacco sticks, plan to furnish a smoking-like involvement in diminished openness to destructive side-effects of ignition.
   Likely Advantages:
   HNB items guarantee to offer a center ground between conventional

cigarettes and complete discontinuance. By warming tobacco at lower temperatures than ignition, these items plan to deliver an inhalable spray with less unsafe synthetic substances. Smokers might find HNB items an elective that holds the ceremonial parts of smoking with possibly lower wellbeing chances.

Difficulties and Exploration Holes:

Research on the security and viability of HNB items is continuous. While they might diminish openness to a few destructive substances, questions stay about the general wellbeing effect and potential for dependence. The business' cases of mischief decrease should be basically assessed through thorough logical request to illuminate proof based general wellbeing arrangements.

3. Smokeless Tobacco Items:

Conventional Smokeless Tobacco:

Smokeless tobacco items, like biting tobacco and snuff, have been utilized for quite a long time. While they accompany their own arrangement of wellbeing chances, including an expanded gamble of oral tumors, some contend that they present a less destructive option in contrast to smoking.

Arising Smokeless Other options:

Advancements in smokeless choices are arising, planning to offer tobacco clients less hurtful choices. These items incorporate snus, a sodden smokeless tobacco item well known in Scandinavia, and other novel details that endeavor to convey nicotine without the hurtful impacts of ignition.

Public Insight and Administrative Difficulties:

The acknowledgment of smokeless tobacco items as mischief decrease apparatuses fluctuates around the world. In locales where smokeless choices are socially acknowledged, they might be all the more promptly embraced. Be that as it may, administrative difficulties, including showcasing limitations and public discernment, should be addressed to guarantee dependable advancement and use.

4. Non-Nicotine Choices:

Home grown and Non-Nicotine Vaping:

Trailblazers are investigating home grown and non-nicotine vaping choices to furnish smokers with options that kill nicotine reliance. Home grown vaping fluids use plant-based fixings, barring nicotine, to make inhalable vapor sprayers. These items expect to reproduce the demonstration of smoking without the habit-forming properties of nicotine.

Potential for Smoking End:

Non-nicotine options might be situated as apparatuses for smoking end, taking care of people who wish to altogether break liberated from nicotine dependence. By giving a recognizable smoking encounter without nicotine, these options focus on the conduct parts of smoking, possibly supporting suspension endeavors.

Administrative Contemplations and Exploration Needs:
As non-nicotine options gain consideration, administrative structures should adjust to address wellbeing, naming, and showcasing concerns. Further exploration is expected to assess the viability of non-nicotine choices in helping smoking end and their general effect on general wellbeing.

5. Imaginative Medication Conveyance Frameworks:
Breathed in Drug Items:
Past nicotine, specialists are investigating breathed in drug items as an original way to deal with drug conveyance. This incorporates inhalable meds for conditions like asthma, persistent obstructive aspiratory infection (COPD), and even antibodies. Breathed in drugs show the potential for hurt decrease by staying away from the requirement for infusion or oral organization.

Double Use and Poly-Use Concerns:
The idea of breathed in drugs raises worries about double use or poly-use, where people might involve these items related to customary tobacco or different substances. Adjusting the helpful capability of breathed in prescriptions with the gamble of potentially negative results requires cautious thought.

6. Exploration and Proof Based Practices:
Logical Thoroughness in Evaluation:
Evaluating the mischief decrease capability of arising advancements and elective items requires logical meticulousness. Powerful exploration systems, including longitudinal investigations, randomized controlled preliminaries, and populace level reviews, are fundamental to assess security, adequacy, and long haul wellbeing results.

Worldwide Cooperation in Exploration:
Given the worldwide idea of the tobacco scourge, joint effort in research is central. Worldwide organizations work with the trading of information, guarantee different points of view are thought of, and add to a more extensive comprehension of the effect of arising innovations on general wellbeing.

7. Difficulties and Contemplations:
Administrative Difficulties and Systems:
Controlling arising innovations and elective items presents difficulties for policymakers. Finding some kind of harmony between cultivating advancement and safeguarding general wellbeing requires

versatile administrative structures that can stay up with the developing scene of tobacco utilization.

Industry Showcasing and Advancement:

Industry showcasing and advancement of arising innovations should be examined to forestall the glamorization of smoking-like ways of behaving and the potential for speaking to youth. Mindful promoting rehearses, combined with clear correspondence of dangers, are fundamental to relieve potentially negative results.

Tending to Double Utilize and Poly-Use:

The potential for double use or poly-utilization of arising items close by customary tobacco entangles hurt decrease systems. Endeavors should be made to grasp examples of purpose, inspirations, and results to illuminate designated mediations that advance mischief decrease without compromising general wellbeing.

Evenhanded Access and Civil rights:

Guaranteeing evenhanded admittance to arising advances and elective items is pivotal to forestall compounding existing wellbeing inconsistencies. Contemplations of reasonableness, accessibility, and social suitability should be coordinated into hurt decrease systems to advance civil rights in tobacco control.

8. Future Bearings:

Interdisciplinary Exploration and Advancement:

The fate of damage decrease in tobacco utilization lies in interdisciplinary exploration and development. Coordinated effort between researchers, medical care experts, designers, policymakers, and social researchers will drive the advancement of successful damage decrease systems that address the intricacy of tobacco use.

Customized Approaches for Assorted Populaces:

Perceiving the variety of tobacco clients and their exceptional requirements, future mischief decrease systems ought to be customized to various populaces. Social, financial, and segment factors should be considered to guarantee that hurt decrease endeavors resound with and really serve different networks.

Coordination with Smoking End Projects:

Arising advances and elective items ought to be incorporated into complete smoking end programs. A comprehensive methodology that consolidates social intercessions, directing, and pharmacotherapy with hurt decrease techniques offers people a range of choices to help their excursion toward a sans smoke life.

Consistent Assessment and Variation:

The powerful idea of the tobacco scene requires persistent assessment and variation of damage decrease methodologies. Continuous observing of arising items, evaluation of their effect on general wellbeing, and acclimations to administrative systems are fundamental parts of a responsive and powerful damage decrease plan.

Investigating arising advances and elective items intended to diminish hurt in tobacco utilization addresses a vital point in the worldwide work to address the wellbeing effects of smoking. From electronic nicotine conveyance frameworks and intensity not-consume items to non-nicotine choices and creative medication conveyance frameworks, the variety of approaches mirrors a promise to finding arrangements that reverberate with different populaces. As social orders explore the intricate territory of mischief decrease, a harmony between development, logical meticulousness, and capable guideline is crucial for shape a future where people have reasonable options that focus on their wellbeing and prosperity on the excursion toward a smoke-liberated world.

9.2 Discuss the controversy and potential benefits of products like e-cigarettes and smokeless tobacco.

The conversation encompassing items like e-cigarettes and smokeless tobacco is set apart by debate and a nuanced assessment of possible advantages and dangers. These elective items have arisen as potential mischief decrease devices, offering smokers choices that expect to diminish openness to unsafe synthetic substances related with customary burnable tobacco. Nonetheless, the continuous discussion depends on logical, moral, and general wellbeing contemplations, as the drawn out impacts and more extensive cultural ramifications keep on being subjects of examination and concern.

E-cigarettes:

The appearance of e-cigarettes, otherwise called electronic nicotine conveyance frameworks (Closures), started critical discussion inside the general wellbeing local area, policymakers, and the overall population. Defenders contend that e-cigarettes give a less unsafe option in contrast to customary smoking, possibly supporting smoking end endeavors. One of the apparent advantages is the shortfall of ignition, which kills the creation of tar and various cancer-causing results related with consuming tobacco. Advocates propose that e-cigarettes address the social parts of smoking, giving a natural hand-to-mouth movement and fulfilling nicotine desires without the destructive impacts of breathing in smoke.

Nonetheless, the discussion encompassing e-cigarettes is multi-layered. Pundits highlight a few key worries, remembering the inadequate exploration for the drawn out wellbeing impacts of breathing in e-cigarette spray. The complicated blend of synthetic substances in e-cigarette fluids, including flavorings and different added substances, brings up issues about likely respiratory and cardiovascular dangers. Besides, the engaging flavors, advertising strategies, and smooth plans of e-cigarettes have been reprimanded for drawing in youth and non-smokers, possibly prompting nicotine habit and resulting tobacco use.

The administrative scene for e-cigarettes has been dynamic, with progressing endeavors to work out some kind of harmony between working with hurt decrease for current smokers and forestalling youth commencement. Clear rules on advertising, flavor limitations, and progress in years confirmation have been proposed to moderate possible damages. The advancing idea of e-cigarette innovation, including the presentation of unit based frameworks and nicotine salts, adds layers of intricacy to administrative difficulties.

Smokeless Tobacco:

Smokeless tobacco items, enveloping different structures like biting tobacco and snuff, have a long history of purpose in specific social settings. Smokeless tobacco is frequently seen as less hurtful than flammable tobacco, basically in light of the fact that it takes out the dangers related with breathing in smoke. Defenders contend that smokeless tobacco gives a mischief decrease choice to people who might battle to stop smoking through different means.

Be that as it may, the likely advantages of smokeless tobacco are tempered by a few contemplations. While smokeless tobacco might decrease the dangers related with respiratory issues, it isn't without wellbeing outcomes. Smokeless tobacco is connected to an expanded gamble of oral malignant growths, gum infection, and other oral medical conditions. The habit-forming nature of nicotine stays a focal worry, as clients of smokeless tobacco items might create and support nicotine reliance.

The social acknowledgment and commonness of smokeless tobacco change generally, with districts like Scandinavia having a long custom of snus use. Conversely, in different areas of the planet, smokeless tobacco might confront disgrace and administrative difficulties. The advertising and advancement of smokeless tobacco items require cautious examination to forestall deluding claims and to guarantee that clients are very much informed about the potential wellbeing chances.

Debates and Difficulties:

The debates encompassing e-cigarettes and smokeless tobacco are interconnected and stretch out past individual wellbeing contemplations. The double difficulties of guaranteeing hurt decrease for current smokers while forestalling inception among non-smokers, especially youth, feature the moral elements of tobacco control endeavors. Finding some kind of harmony between empowering smokers to change to possibly less hurtful other options and forestalling the entrenchment of nicotine dependence among new clients is a perplexing undertaking.

One of the focal discussions is the potential for these elective items to renormalize smoking ways of behaving. The captivating flavors, careful plans, and promoting systems utilized by producers might add to making smoking-like ways of behaving socially adequate or even trendy. This raises worries about the possible disintegration of many years of progress in denormalizing smoking and cultivating a without smoke culture.

Besides, the impact of the tobacco business in molding the story around these items is a tenacious concern. Industry strategies, including forceful advertising and campaigning endeavors, have generally sabotaged general wellbeing drives. Doubt about the inspirations driving advancing elective items is justified, given the business' verifiable history of focusing on benefits over general wellbeing.

Likely Advantages:

While debates persevere, recognizing the possible advantages of these elective items is pivotal for an exhaustive comprehension of damage decrease techniques. For people who have battled to stop smoking utilizing customary techniques, e-cigarettes and smokeless tobacco might offer a scaffold toward diminished hurt. A few examinations propose that people who change to smokeless tobacco or e-cigarettes experience a decline in openness to hurtful substances tracked down in burnable tobacco.

With regards to smoking suspension, these choices might act as temporary devices, permitting people to bit by bit lessen their reliance on nicotine and, now and again, quit smoking by and large. Social mediations, joined with the utilization of elective items, structure some portion of thorough smoking end programs that address both the physiological and mental parts of fixation.

The potential advantages likewise reach out to general wellbeing contemplations. In the event that countless smokers progress to less unsafe other options, there could be a decrease in smoking-related sicknesses and medical services costs. Hurt decrease techniques, when executed mindfully and morally, can possibly save lives and work on the general wellbeing of populaces.

Difficult exercise and Future Contemplations:

Exploring the intricacies of damage decrease with regards to e-cigarettes and smokeless tobacco requires a sensitive difficult exercise. Policymakers, general wellbeing authorities, and scientists should gauge the expected advantages for current smokers against the dangers of re-standardization and youth commencement. Administrative structures need to advance to address the developing scene of elective tobacco items, consolidating proof based measures that focus on general wellbeing.

The future contemplations for hurt decrease systems include proceeded with examination to fill holes in how we might interpret the wellbeing impacts of these items. Longitudinal examinations, populace level investigations, and reconnaissance of patterns are fundamental parts of proof based policymaking. The improvement of clear correspondence systems to teach the general population about the dangers and advantages of elective items is basic, underscoring straightforwardness and countering industry-driven stories.

Moreover, hurt decrease systems should be coordinated into more extensive tobacco control endeavors that envelop counteraction, suspension, and strategy drives. Far reaching approaches that address the financial determinants of tobacco use, battle industry impact, and cultivate a strong climate for smoking discontinuance are fundamental for the progress of damage decrease drives.

Proceeding with the conversation on the discussion and possible advantages of items like e-cigarettes and smokeless tobacco requires a more profound investigation of explicit regions like public discernment, administrative difficulties, hurt decrease as a general wellbeing procedure, and the job of industry in forming these stories.

Public Discernment and Conduct Elements:

Public discernment assumes a significant part in forming the achievement or disappointment of mischief decrease procedures including items like e-cigarettes and smokeless tobacco. The double idea of these items as potential mischief decrease instruments and as wellsprings of new wellbeing chances entangles how they are seen by people and networks.

One part of public insight spins around the idea of mischief decrease itself. Some contend that hurt decrease, as a commonsense way to deal with relieve the dangers related with customary smoking, lines up with the rule of meeting people where they are in their excursion toward stopping. Others, notwithstanding, express worries that embracing hurt decrease may incidentally support proceeded with nicotine use and thwart more extensive smoking discontinuance endeavors.

The conduct elements of tobacco use and end further convolute public insight. The charm of recognizable ceremonies, like the demonstration of smoking or the utilization of smokeless tobacco, can be strong forces to be reckoned with. Conduct dependence on the ceremonies related with smoking, past the dependence on drugs to nicotine, may present difficulties to those endeavoring to stop. In this specific situation, hurt decrease systems recognize and address the social parts of fixation, perceiving that stopping is a complicated cycle impacted by both physiological and mental elements.

Administrative Difficulties and Moral Contemplations:

Exploring the administrative scene of elective tobacco items is laden with difficulties that stretch out past logical and wellbeing contemplations. Administrative bodies should wrestle with the fragile harmony between cultivating development, safeguarding general wellbeing, and forestalling likely damage.

The advancing idea of these items, combined with forceful advertising strategies, requires versatile structures that can stay up with industry advancements.One significant administrative test is laying out a system that supports development for hurt decrease while successfully diminishing youth inception and forestalling the re-standardization of smoking ways of behaving. Finding some kind of harmony includes contemplations of showcasing limitations, flavor boycotts, age confirmation measures, and clear correspondence of dangers.

The moral elements of administrative choices are foremost. Policymakers should gauge the expected advantages for current smokers against the dangers of captivating non-smokers, especially youth, into a long lasting propensity for nicotine use. Straightforwardness, logical honesty, and a guarantee to general wellbeing ought to direct administrative choices, guaranteeing that hurt decrease systems line up with more extensive tobacco control targets.

Hurt Decrease as a General Wellbeing System:

Hurt decrease, as a general wellbeing procedure, incorporates a realistic way to deal with address the mind boggling difficulties of tobacco use. Perceiving that not all people will or can stop tobacco use right away, hurt decrease tries to limit the unfriendly wellbeing results related with smoking while at the same time giving pathways to possible end.

With regards to e-cigarettes and smokeless tobacco, hurt decrease techniques recognize that a few people might find it trying to suddenly stop nicotine. By offering choices that lessen openness to destructive burning results, hurt decrease intends to make a continuum of care that obliges different inclinations and status to stop.

The likely advantages of damage decrease reach out past individual wellbeing results to more extensive general wellbeing contemplations. On the off chance that a significant number of smokers change to less destructive other options, there could be a decrease in smoking-related illnesses and related medical care costs. Hurt decrease systems, when carried out dependably, can add to further developed populace wellbeing results and make an establishment for supported tobacco control endeavors.

Notwithstanding, the progress of damage decrease as a general wellbeing methodology depends on a few key variables. Powerful correspondence of dangers and advantages, clear rules for item principles, and ceaseless assessment of the effect of mischief decrease drives are fundamental parts.

In addition, the combination of damage decrease into extensive tobacco control programs guarantees that these procedures supplement more extensive endeavors to forestall commencement, advance discontinuance, and address financial determinants of tobacco use.

Industry Impact and Corporate Obligation:

The job of the tobacco business in forming the story around e-cigarettes and smokeless tobacco acquaints a layer of intricacy with the discussion. By and large, the business has been condemned for focusing on benefits over general wellbeing, utilizing forceful showcasing strategies, and endeavoring to sabotage tobacco control measures.

With regards to elective items, the business' inspirations and strategies warrant investigation. The showcasing of e-cigarettes, specifically, has been described by smooth plans, alluring flavors, and publicizing that reverberations prior methodologies used to advance customary cigarettes. The potential for these items to act as a passage to customary smoking, particularly among youth, raises moral worries about industry rehearses.

Corporate obligation turns into an essential thought in this unique situation. Capable advertising that abstains from glamorizing smoking-like ways of behaving, clear correspondence of dangers, and adherence to guidelines are basic for relieving possible damages. Cooperative endeavors between the business, administrative bodies, and general wellbeing advocates are fundamental to guarantee that hurt decrease techniques are carried out in a way that focuses on general wellbeing over corporate interests.

The Convergence of Civil rights and General Wellbeing:

Inspecting the debate and possible advantages of items like e-cigarettes and smokeless tobacco additionally requires an investigation of their convergence with civil rights contemplations. Tobacco use has generally been connected to abberations in view of financial variables, race, and training. The presentation of elective items brings up issues about how these abberations might be sustained or tended to.

Guaranteeing evenhanded admittance to hurt decrease devices is a pivotal part of civil rights in tobacco control. Differences in access, affected by elements like pay and geographic area, should be effectively addressed to forestall the worsening of existing wellbeing imbalances. General wellbeing drives ought to be planned with social awareness, perceiving that various networks might have fluctuated impression of damage decrease and elective tobacco items.

Moreover, regard for the expected effect of industry promoting on weak populaces is fundamental. Networks with generally higher paces of tobacco use might be lopsidedly impacted by industry strategies, requiring designated intercessions to balance likely damages.

All in all, the debate and possible advantages of items like e-cigarettes and smokeless tobacco typify the intricacy of mischief decrease in the more extensive setting of tobacco control. Public discernment, administrative difficulties, moral contemplations, industry impact, and civil rights cross in a complex scene where individual wellbeing decisions resonate across networks and populaces.

Exploring this scene requires a pledge to confirm based policymaking, straightforwardness, and a comprehensive comprehension of the elements that impact tobacco use. Hurt decrease, as a general wellbeing procedure, should be incorporated into complete tobacco control endeavors that address both the individual and cultural components of tobacco-related hurt.

As social orders keep on wrestling with developing innovations and moving inclinations, the basic is to find an equilibrium that focuses on general wellbeing over industry interests, shields weak populaces, and encourages a steady climate for people on their excursion toward a sans smoke life. The continuous discussion and dynamic nature of the field highlight the requirement for ceaseless examination, smart policymaking, and an aggregate obligation to understanding a future where the staggering effects of tobacco use are essentially relieved.

All in all, the contentions and potential advantages encompassing items like e-cigarettes and smokeless tobacco highlight the requirement for a nuanced, proof based way to deal with hurt decrease in tobacco control. As social orders wrestle with developing advances and moving inclinations, moral contemplations, administrative structures, and general wellbeing needs should adjust to guarantee that hurt decrease techniques add to the all-encompassing objective of diminishing the staggering effect of tobacco use on individual and general wellbeing.

Chapter 10

Towards a Smoke-Free Future

Towards a Without smoke Future: Exploring Difficulties and Embracing Developments

The vision of a without smoke future addresses a groundbreaking worldview in worldwide general wellbeing, rising above the customary ways to deal with tobacco control. As social orders wrestle with the staggering wellbeing results of smoking, imaginative procedures and far reaching drives are arising to prepare toward a future where the commonness of smoking is fundamentally diminished, on the off chance that not destroyed. This talk dives into the complex scene of difficulties, valuable open doors, and imaginative mediations that by and large add to the goal of a sans smoke future.

1. The Worldwide Weight of Smoking:
   The study of disease transmission and Wellbeing Effects:
   Smoking remaining parts a worldwide general wellbeing challenge, adding to a significant weight of illness.
   The World Wellbeing Association (WHO) gauges that tobacco use is liable for in excess of 8 million passings every year, with immediate and handed-down cigarette smoke openness connected to a scope of illnesses, including cardiovascular circumstances, respiratory sicknesses, and different diseases. Addressing this stunning cost requires a purposeful work to rethink cultural standards around tobacco use.
   Financial Abberations:
   The effect of smoking stretches out past wellbeing results, sustaining financial incongruities. Weak populaces frequently bear an unbalanced weight, confronting higher paces of tobacco use and

decreased admittance to smoking discontinuance assets. The excursion towards a without smoke future requires systems that focus on the physiological parts of fixation as well as address the social determinants that add to tobacco use differences.

2. Hurt Decrease Methodologies:

Job of Elective Items:

Embracing hurt decrease methodologies addresses a vital part of the guide towards a sans smoke future. Elective items, like e-cigarettes and smokeless tobacco, certainly stand out for their capability to give less hurtful options in contrast to conventional smoking. The contention encompassing these items highlights the requirement for proof based assessments of their part in hurt decrease, recognizing both possible advantages and dangers.

Challenges in Execution:

Executing hurt decrease techniques faces difficulties on numerous fronts. Administrative structures should work out some kind of harmony between cultivating development and forestalling potentially negative side-effects, like youth commencement. Tending to public discernment, industry impact, and moral contemplations is fundamental to guaranteeing that hurt decrease lines up with more extensive tobacco control targets.

3. Developments in Smoking Suspension:

Social Mediations:

Social mediations assume a significant part in smoking discontinuance endeavors. From guiding and support gatherings to advanced stages and versatile applications, imaginative methodologies influence brain research, innovation, and local area commitment to engage people on their excursion to stop smoking. The reconciliation of conduct intercessions into medical care frameworks and local area settings is fundamental to extending admittance to discontinuance support.

Pharmacotherapy Progressions:

Progressions in pharmacotherapy offer people a range of choices to help with smoking suspension. From nicotine substitution treatments to novel prescriptions focusing on the brain processes related with habit, research in pharmacological mediations proceeds to refine and extend the tool stash accessible to medical care experts and people trying to stop smoking.

4. Mechanical Arrangements:

Computerized Wellbeing Mediations:

The computerized period has introduced another influx of smoking discontinuance mediations. Portable applications, virtual care groups, and telehealth administrations give open and customized assets to people hoping to stop smoking. The coordination of information investigation and man-made brainpower upgrades the fitting of intercessions, further developing adequacy and reach.

Arising Advancements:

Past customary methodologies, arising advances offer novel answers for smoking discontinuance. Computer generated reality treatments, sensor-based observing gadgets, and, surprisingly, wearable innovations add to a more far reaching comprehension of smoking ways of behaving and give continuous input, expanding conventional discontinuance systems.

5. Social and Social Movements:

De-normalizing Smoking:

Moving social standards and de-normalizing smoking ways of behaving are central to accomplishing a without smoke future. Far reaching general wellbeing efforts, local area drives, and strategy measures add to changing cultural insights around tobacco use. The accentuation on depicting smoking as socially inadmissible is a foundation of these endeavors.

Youth Counteraction and Instruction:

Putting resources into youth counteraction and schooling is a proactive technique chasing a sans smoke future. Far reaching school-based programs, local area exceed, and designated crusades address the one of a kind difficulties presented by the tobacco business' promoting strategies and forestall the inception of tobacco use among youngsters.

6. Worldwide Joint effort and Information Trade:

Global Participation:

The worldwide idea of the tobacco pandemic highlights the significance of global cooperation. Information trade, sharing prescribed procedures, and adjusting methodologies on a worldwide scale add to an aggregate exertion that rises above lines and addresses the interconnected difficulties of tobacco control.

Tending to Financial Determinants:

Perceiving the financial determinants of tobacco use, future endeavors ought to address fundamental variations. Battling tobacco-related wellbeing disparities requires an extensive methodology that thinks about friendly, financial, and ecological elements, planning to make conditions that help without tobacco ways of life.

7. Local area Commitment and Strengthening:

Neighborhood Drives and Grassroots Developments:

Enabling people group to play a functioning job in tobacco control encourages practical change. Local area drove drives, grassroots preparation, and the inclusion of different partners add to a feeling of pride and obligation, enhancing the effect of tobacco control endeavors.

Advancement in Exploration and Assessment:

Progressing examination and assessment endeavors are fundamental for remaining in front of arising patterns and refining tobacco control techniques. Advancement in research approaches, information examination, and assessment structures upgrades the proof base, directing the improvement of compelling mediations and arrangements.

All in all, the excursion towards a sans smoke future is set apart by the combination of different methodologies, difficulties, and developments. From hurt decrease drives and smoking discontinuance headways to mechanical arrangements, social movements, and worldwide joint effort, the diverse methodology mirrors a promise to reshaping the direction of tobacco use.

The worldwide local area's aggregate endeavors should stretch out past ordinary strategies, embracing the unique scene of advancements and tending to the financial determinants that fuel tobacco use. As society explores the intricacies of a sans smoke future, the collaboration of general wellbeing drives, mechanical headways, and local area strengthening will assume a vital part in understanding an existence where the staggering effects of smoking are fundamentally reduced. The persistent quest for proof based techniques, informed by a promise to value and worldwide cooperation, holds the way to accomplishing the extraordinary vision of a without smoke future for a long time into the future.

10.1 Summarize the progress made in reducing tobacco use globally.

The worldwide endeavors to lessen tobacco use have seen huge advancement throughout the long term, mirroring a diverse methodology that joins strategy mediations, general wellbeing efforts, mechanical developments, and cooperative drives. This complete undertaking points not exclusively to diminish the commonness of smoking yet additionally to address the related wellbeing, social, and monetary weights. As we dive into the headway made in diminishing tobacco use universally, it is fundamental to consider the different components of this complex test and the procedures utilized to battle it.

The World Wellbeing Association's (WHO) Structure Show on Tobacco Control (FCTC) remains as a foundation in the global obligation to checking tobacco use. Taken on in 2003, the FCTC addresses a worldwide settlement that gives a strong structure to nations to carry out proof based tobacco control measures. The deal envelops a large number of systems, including tax collection, without smoke strategies, bundling and marking guidelines, promoting boycotts, and backing for smoking end programs. The far and wide confirmation of the FCTC exhibits a worldwide agreement on the criticalness of tending to the tobacco pestilence.

One of the critical accomplishments in diminishing tobacco use worldwide is the far and wide reception of exhaustive tobacco control strategies at the public level. Numerous nations have carried out tough tobacco control measures lined up with FCTC rules. Sans smoke regulations, which limit smoking in broad daylight spaces and work environments, have become more pervasive, adding to a decrease in openness to handed-down cigarette smoke. Moreover, realistic admonition marks on cigarette bundles have become norm in numerous locales, filling in as a visual obstacle and giving data on the wellbeing gambles related with smoking.

Tobacco tax collection has shown to be an integral asset in diminishing tobacco utilization. Numerous nations have carried out significant expansions in tobacco charges, prompting more exorbitant costs for tobacco items. This has not just gone about as a hindrance for likely smokers yet has likewise been powerful in empowering current smokers to stop. The monetary reasoning behind tobacco tax assessment lies in the guideline of cost flexibility, where greater costs connect with diminished request.

Besides, public mindfulness crusades play had a significant impact in forming cultural perspectives towards tobacco use. Legislatures, non-administrative associations, and worldwide bodies have sent off significant missions to instruct people in general about the wellbeing dangers of smoking, the advantages of suspension, and the more extensive cultural results of tobacco use. These missions use different media stations, including TV, radio, virtual entertainment, and public occasions, to arrive at assorted populaces and scatter against smoking messages.

Mechanical developments have likewise contributed essentially to the advancement in lessening tobacco use. Computerized wellbeing intercessions, like portable applications and online stages, give available and customized assets to smoking suspension. These computerized devices offer elements like quit plans, progress following, and social help, taking care of the advancing inclinations and ways of life of people looking to stop smoking.

The worldwide advancement in decreasing tobacco use isn't just about checking the interest for tobacco items yet in addition about addressing the perplexing snare of variables that add to tobacco utilization. Financial determinants, social impacts, and industry strategies are fundamental parts of this diverse test. Endeavors to lessen tobacco use worldwide perceive the need to handle these fundamental variables to make maintainable, long haul change.

Regardless of these headways
challenges persevere, and the tobacco scene keeps on advancing. One of the continuous difficulties is the forceful promoting strategies utilized by the tobacco business. The business has a long history of adjusting to evolving conditions, tracking down better approaches to showcase its items and keep up with benefit. While huge steps have been made in limiting tobacco publicizing and sponsorship, the business consistently looks for provisos and elective roads to advance its items, particularly focusing on weak populaces and developing business sectors.

One more test lies in the rise of novel tobacco and nicotine items, frequently promoted as choices or diminished hurt items. Electronic cigarettes (e-cigarettes), warmed tobacco items, and other smokeless choices have acquired prominence, introducing the two amazing open doors and dangers in the journey to lessen tobacco use. The discussion encompassing these items spins around their likely job in hurt decrease for current smokers versus the gamble of tempting non-smokers, especially youth, into nicotine dependence.

The impact of the tobacco business stretches out past advertising strategies to prosecution procedures pointed toward testing and deferring tobacco control measures. Fights in court over issues like advance notice marks, bundling guidelines, and promoting limitations show the business' persevering endeavors to sabotage general wellbeing drives. Beating these lawful difficulties requires a strong and versatile administrative structure that expects industry moves and stays zeroed in on safeguarding general wellbeing.

Furthermore, worldwide differences in tobacco control endeavors stay a worry. While major league salary nations have gained significant headway in diminishing tobacco use, low-and center pay nations face novel difficulties, including restricted assets, feeble administrative foundations, and the effect of tobacco industry strategies. Connecting these worldwide inconsistencies requires coordinated endeavors to offer help, assets, and information move to less monetarily advantaged locales.

The headway made in lessening tobacco use around the world is likewise complicatedly connected to more extensive general wellbeing contemplations. The conjunction of tobacco use with other gamble factors, like horrible eating routine, actual dormancy, and liquor utilization, highlights the requirement for incorporated ways to deal with address various wellbeing determinants all the while. Complete general wellbeing methodologies that envelop a range of chance elements add to by and large upgrades in populace wellbeing and prosperity.

Looking forward, the direction toward a without smoke future requires nonstop development and variation. The quick development of the tobacco scene, combined with arising difficulties and open doors, requires a dynamic and responsive methodology. Examination and reconnaissance endeavors should remain in front of new turns of events, assessing the effect of arising items, evaluating industry strategies, and illuminating proof based approaches.

Worldwide coordinated effort stays vital chasing a without smoke future. Information trade, shared assets, and cooperative examination drives empower nations to gain from one another's triumphs and difficulties. Worldwide associations, like the WHO, assume a focal part in planning these cooperative endeavors, giving direction, and encouraging an aggregate obligation to tobacco control.

All in all, the headway made in diminishing tobacco use universally mirrors a striking aggregate exertion that traverses strategy, general wellbeing, innovation, and local area commitment. The far and wide reception of extensive tobacco control measures, public mindfulness crusades, tax collection methodologies, and mechanical developments has added to a decrease in smoking rates and an expanded spotlight on making a tobacco-liberated world.

In any case, the excursion is nowhere near finished, and challenges endure as industry strategies, arising items, fights in court, and worldwide abberations. Supporting and speeding up progress requires a cautious and versatile methodology that tends to the developing scene of tobacco use. A definitive objective of accomplishing a without smoke future requests proceeded with cooperation, development, and an immovable obligation to focusing on general wellbeing over industry interests. As social orders explore this perplexing landscape, the vision of a world liberated from the overwhelming wellbeing outcomes of tobacco use stays a main impetus for continuous endeavors and worldwide cooperation.

10.2 Explore future trends and potential solutions to create a smoke-free world.

Investigating what's to come patterns and likely answers for make a smoke-liberated world includes digging into a unique scene molded by mechanical progressions, developing cultural mentalities, administrative developments, and cooperative endeavors. As we look into the future, the vision of a smoke-liberated world isn't just optimistic however requires a vital and exhaustive way to deal with explore the difficulties and jump all over the chances that lie ahead.

1. Mechanical Advancements in Smoking Discontinuance:
    The fate of smoking discontinuance is complicatedly attached to mechanical developments that influence the force of computerized wellbeing intercessions. Versatile applications, computer generated

reality treatments, and wearable innovations are supposed to assume a pivotal part in giving customized and open assets to people looking to stop smoking. These advancements offer continuous criticism, intuitive emotionally supportive networks, and information driven experiences that improve the adequacy of suspension endeavors. The joining of man-made brainpower (simulated intelligence) may additionally fit mediations to individual inclinations and ways of behaving, introducing another period of accuracy medication in smoking end.

2. Hurt Decrease Methodologies:
   The investigation of mischief decrease systems keeps on being a critical pattern in the journey for a smoke-liberated world. Elective nicotine conveyance frameworks, like e-cigarettes and warmed to-bacco items, have acquired conspicuousness as possible devices for diminishing mischief related with customary smoking. Be that as it may, the continuous discussion encompassing these items requires powerful examination, clear guidelines, and watchful checking of industry practices to guarantee they truly add to hurt decrease without incidentally cultivating new conditions, particularly among youth.

3. Administrative Developments and Strategy Measures:
   Future patterns in tobacco control will probably observe a proceeded with development of administrative systems and strategy measures. The viability of existing approaches, like tax assessment, sans smoke regulations, and promoting limitations, will be assessed, with an accentuation on adjusting to arising difficulties. Developments in strategy might remember stricter guidelines for arising items, novel ways to deal with counter industry strategies, and the mix of con-duct financial aspects standards to impact smoking way of behaving. The administrative scene should stay lithe to address the advancing idea of the tobacco business and its systems.

4. Worldwide Cooperation and Information Trade:
   The worldwide idea of the tobacco scourge highlights the signifi-cance of proceeded with global cooperation and information trade. Future patterns are probably going to see upgraded coordination between nations, global associations, and general wellbeing advo-cates. The sharing of best practices, examples learned, and explore discoveries can work with an aggregate reaction to challenges and speed up progress toward a smoke-liberated world. Drives that focus on supporting low-and center pay nations in their tobacco control endeavors will be vital for accomplishing value in worldwide tobacco control.

5. **Conduct Intercessions and Local area Commitment:**
   The eventual fate of smoking discontinuance will keep on under-scoring conduct mediations and local area commitment as essential parts of thorough tobacco control procedures. Socially delicate projects, local area drove drives, and designated intercessions customized to different populaces will address the financial determinants of tobacco use. Enabling people group to play a functioning job in tobacco control cultivates manageable change and adds to the de-standardization of smoking, reshaping cultural standards and assumptions.

6. **Tending to Industry Strategies and Lawful Difficulties:**
   Expecting and tending to industry strategies will stay a basic part of making a smoke-liberated world. As the tobacco scene advances, so do the procedures utilized by the business to evade guidelines and keep up with piece of the pie. Future patterns might include uplifted examination of industry showcasing, counter-advertising drives, and legitimate measures to forestall obstruction in general wellbeing approaches. Watchfulness against legitimate difficulties is pivotal, requiring strong administrative structures that endure industry pressures and focus on general wellbeing goals.

7. **General Wellbeing Efforts and Instruction:**
   Future patterns in tobacco control will observer a continuous obligation to general wellbeing efforts and training. Inventive missions utilizing online entertainment, forces to be reckoned with, and customized informing will target explicit socioeconomics, stressing the drawn out wellbeing results of smoking and the advantages of discontinuance. Training programs in schools and networks will assume a critical part in forestalling youth commencement and cultivating a without tobacco culture, making a generational change in perspectives towards smoking.

8. **Arising Advances and Elective Items:**
   The investigation of arising advances and elective items will shape the future scene of tobacco control. Nonstop examination into the wellbeing and adequacy of new items will illuminate administrative choices, guaranteeing that hurt decrease procedures are proof based. The likely rise of novel non-nicotine choices and forward leaps in pharmacotherapy may give extra choices to people hoping to stop smoking, adding to an enhanced tool stash for smoking discontinuance.

9. **Financial Contemplations and Wellbeing Value:**
   Future patterns in tobacco control will focus on tending to financial determinants and wellbeing value. Perceiving that tobacco use

excessively influences weak populaces, endeavors will be guided towards diminishing variations in admittance to discontinuance assets, carrying out strategies that think about the financial effect on minimized networks, and encouraging social conditions that help smoking end.

10. Exploration and Reconnaissance:

The eventual fate of tobacco control depends vigorously on proceeded with examination and observation. Strong examinations on the wellbeing impacts of arising items, assessment of strategy adequacy, and investigation of industry strategies will give the proof base to informed navigation. Reconnaissance frameworks should adjust to screen evolving patterns, distinguish arising difficulties, and guide the iterative advancement of tobacco control techniques.

All in all, investigating future patterns and possible answers for make a smoke-liberated world requires an all encompassing and dynamic methodology that adjusts to the developing idea of the tobacco scene. The cooperative energy of mechanical developments, administrative progressions, worldwide joint effort, and local area strengthening will be crucial in molding a future where the staggering wellbeing outcomes of tobacco use are essentially moderated. The vision of a smoke-liberated world isn't just an aggressive objective yet an aggregate basic that requests continuous devotion, development, and a resolute obligation to focusing on general wellbeing over industry interests.